OFF
THE
BENCH
AND INTO THE GAME

OFF THE BENCH

AND INTO THE GAME

EIGHT SUCCESS STRATEGIES FROM PROFESSIONAL SPORT

Ryan Walter

VICTORIA · VANCOUVER · CALGARY

Heritage House Publishing Company Ltd.
#108 – 17665 66A Avenue
Surrey, BC V3S 2A7
www.heritagehouse.ca

Heritage House Publishing Company Ltd.
P.O. Box 468
Custer, WA
98240-0468

LIBRARY AND ARCHIVES CANADA CATALOGUING IN PUBLICATION

Walter, Ryan, 1958–
     Off the bench and into the game: eight success strategies from professional sport / Ryan Walter.—Updated and expanded.

Includes bibliographical references.
ISBN 13: 978-1-894974-23-3; ISBN 10: 1-894974-23-9

     1. Success. 2. Leadership. 3. Achievement motivation.
4. Sports—Psychological aspects. I. Title.

BF637.S8W34 2006   158.1   C2006-904175-X

LIBRARY OF CONGRESS CONTROL NUMBER: 2006932767

Cover design by Jacqui Thomas
Interior design by Jennifer Lippa
Front-cover photo courtesy of Delicious Photography
Back-cover and interior photos courtesy of Ryan and Jenn Walter unless otherwise noted

Printed in Canada

Heritage House acknowledges the financial support for its publishing program from the Government of Canada through the Book Publishing Industry Development Program (BPIDP), Canada Council for the Arts, and the province of British Columbia through the British Columbia Arts Council and the Book Publishing Tax Credit.

I want to dedicate this book first to four people I love and respect:
my mom and dad, Viona and Bill, and Jenn's parents, Florence and George.
You have lived these principles. This is about you.

Second, to my six closest friends on earth, who make my life:
our children, Ben, Christy, Ryan, Joe and Emma, and my best friend
and life partner, Jenn. This is for you.

Finally, to our Heavenly Father. This is from you.

Contents

Foreword

I have been involved in the great sport of hockey for most of my life. During this time I have had the pleasure of meeting many fine people. Ryan Walter has long been admired for his positive contributions to the game of hockey, and I consider him one of my very closest friends. I have been his teammate as well as his opponent and admired the dedication with which he approached the game. I can now admire that same dedication in his approach to living successfully after the game.

In *Off the Bench and Into the Game*, Ryan has taken many of the true principles of professional sport and applied them to everyday life. As an athlete, I always believed that many of the disciplines I learned in hockey could be useful in life both away from the rink and after my playing career was completed. Ryan has accomplished the task of summarizing these positive attributes in a simple and straightforward manner.

His eight strategies are a very accurate representation of what it takes to be successful not only in athletics but also away from the game. The idea of "failing forward" that Ryan describes in Chapter 7 is truly one that should be embraced. We all fail at times, but it is what we do after we fail that sets our future course. I also enjoyed the many humorous stories that Ryan uses, even at his own expense, to reinforce the principles that he conveys. His use of numerous quotes from such historical icons as Winston Churchill, Abraham Lincoln and Mark Twain adds depth to the ideas he puts before the reader.

Ryan has accomplished the task of taking attributes that he has learned in the world of professional sports and transferring them to everyday life. *Off the Bench and Into the Game* is an insightful book and a great read.

—Mike Gartner, NHL star, 1979–98

Ryan Walter, Vancouver Canucks, 1991–93.

Warm-up **Preparing to Perform**

HOCKEY IS THE GREATEST GAME IN THE WORLD. I've been passionately connected with it since the age of seven, first as an amateur, junior and professional player and later as a coach, owner and broadcaster. Who would have thought the day my father signed me up for minor hockey that it would become such a huge part of the rest of my life?

And who would have thought that the game of hockey would have so much to teach me about life? Sports somehow speed up life's learning curve. We see the results of our preparation, performance and team play instantaneously with a win, loss or tie. My 15 highly competitive years in the National Hockey League, and the long process of getting there, gave me a heightened awareness of the importance of competition, motivation, self-worth, performance and accomplishment. I want to share this with you. As I reflect on some of the success strategies I learned from the sports world, and hockey specifically, my hope is that these personal stories and applied principles move life's benchwarmers into the heart of the action and give every player a chance at peak performance.

The first four chapters deal with areas of our lives over which we have control. Tinkering with the way we think, talk, focus and perform can bring us the life success that we all desire. Change starts with us! Chapters 5 and 6 explore facets of the term "team," for each of us performs within team cultures in some area of our lives. Everyone has their own picture of how a team player and leader should look, act and react. I'd like to give you my take on "team," based on real-life examples from the world of sports and personal experience.

Chapter 7 will introduce the most important success principle that I know—"failing forward." The key to winning always includes a large dose of perseverance! The goal of Chapter 8 is to bring it all together into one thought ... now what? Bernard "Tiny" Freyberg, the great Second World War general, voiced one of my favourite thoughts: "You can't treat a man like a butler and expect him to fight like a gladiator." This statement is also true in how we treat ourselves. Information has power when applied with the desire to make personal change. At the end of this book we desire our *hero* (you) to take action! Our final chapter, "Be a Hero," empowers you to make a difference in someone's life tomorrow. Finally, we will end our time together in "overtime," entering an NHL dressing room to pull our team together and then send it out to compete for the championship.

If there is one thing that all hockey players have in common, regardless of age or talent, it's practice. After the biggest win of his life, a player still goes to practice the next day because the goal is always to learn more and get better. Whether you find yourself in the heat of the action right now or watching from the sidelines, I encourage you to allow these next pages to build your confidence and possibly change your approach as you work toward achieving your goals.

Frederick Handley Page was an aviator during the early days of flight. Flying over the North African desert, Page heard a disturbing gnawing noise directly behind his seat. The sound increased, and he realized that it must have been coming from a rat that had smelled his box lunch and jumped on the plane during refuelling. What was Page to do? His major concern was the plane's hydraulic line, which ran behind his seat. If the rat were to puncture any part of the line, he would be in big trouble. Page did not have an automatic pilot or copilot, so chasing the rat with a big stick was not an option. He began to rack his brain. Suddenly he remembered a trivial and seemingly insignificant piece of information: He had once read that rats need more oxygen to live than humans, and he reasoned that if he could get to a higher altitude where there is less oxygen in the air, the rat would die. So he pulled back on the stick and soared as high as he dared. The gnawing stopped. Page landed a little while later and found a very large, dead rat, inches away from the hydraulic line.

So what's the significance of this story, you ask? It has been my experience that when we apply small amounts of critical information at crucial times in our lives, the results can be life-changing. So here we go! Let's get off the bench and into the game ... or sit there if you want ... the choice is yours.

 If you take care of the small things, the big things take care of themselves. You can gain more control over your life by paying closer attention to the little things.

—Emily Dickinson, American poet

Ryan early in his NHL career with the Washington Capitals.

Chapter 1 **Be Mentally Tough: Choose Successful Habits of Thought**

Confidence is: Going after Moby Dick in a rowboat, and taking the tartar sauce with you; a Bullfighter who goes in the ring with mustard on his sword.

—Zig Ziglar, *How to Be A Winner*

MY NATIONAL HOCKEY LEAGUE CAREER began in Washington, D.C., with the Washington Capitals. I was drafted Number 2 in the world in 1978 and played my first NHL season that same year. These were the days of the tough, intimidating Philadelphia Flyers, who had won two Stanley Cups with their very aggressive style of play. Our Capitals met the Flyers often, as we were in the same division. They played a brand of hockey that used intimidation to steal an advantage over their opponents. As I look back on those years, the advantage that the Flyers created for themselves with their intimidating image was not necessarily a reality on the ice. The Flyers' advantage came from instilling doubt and fear of what might happen into the minds of opposing teams. Their reputation for being a mean, brawling team preceded them and many times succeeded in keeping the opposing teams on edge. Teams coming to play the "Broad Street Bullies" at the old Spectrum arena often arrived with knots in their stomachs and nervous tension in their dressing rooms.

Playing against tough NHL teams and players taught me this: mental toughness comes by choosing—through an act of our will—to control the thoughts on which we allow ourselves to dwell. I found that my courage would melt when I allowed my mind to think ahead toward some negative thing that very seldom actually happened. I also realized that when I chose to take control of my thinking, I more often than not could create the desired action or attitude.

Preparing for a match against the Flyers in the Spectrum involved learning to think and say the right things. We did not allow our minds to wander toward, "I wonder how things will go tonight? Will I have someone coming after me? I wish this game were next week! I'm having trouble with my game this week." We learned to *change our minds*! We would tell each other before the game, "The Philadelphia Flyers put their pants on one leg at a time, boys!" In other words, we were reminding one another that the players on their team were not superhuman, but the same as us.

 What lies behind us and what lies before us are tiny matters, compared to what lies within us.

—Ralph Waldo Emerson, American philosopher and poet

Confidence and mental toughness grow when we choose to control the thoughts on which we allow ourselves to dwell. Before many games, I remember forcing myself to think thoughts that would build my mental toughness, courage and competitiveness. I would constantly say, "I have no fear of any players at any time, anywhere. I have in the past, and will in the future, compete against the toughest players in the NHL, and enjoy doing it. Not only will

I be the very best that I can be in tonight's game, but no player on the opposing team is going to get in my way."

I learned early in my hockey career that players, and people in general, are not born with courage or fearlessness or competitiveness. These important qualities develop in our minds over time. Successful athletes realize that they must steer their thoughts like a ship, or they will not reach their desired destination.

Almost all success begins by first building our confidence and developing mental toughness

The first step toward creating real, positive, impacting change must start with disciplining our thoughts. Many of us have learned the hard way the damage that can be done by giving negative thoughts a place in our minds. I heard the story of a very healthy man who was scheduled for a routine prostate operation at a local hospital. After surgery, he was rolled on a stretcher into the wrong room, and the doctor consequently came in with the wrong file for this man. The doctor began in no uncertain terms to tell this man that, while performing his surgery, they had found a serious heart condition, as well as cancer. The man went home in shock, and he died that evening of heart failure. Most athletes have learned the debilitating power of worry first-hand. It quickly fosters a lack of confidence that can sabotage the best intentions and greatest talents. Worry is undisciplined thinking that harms our ambitions and our lives.

DEVELOPING OUR MENTAL TOUGHNESS MUSCLE

One day after practice I asked Peter Twist, at the time the well-respected strength and conditioning coach of the NHL's Vancouver Canucks, "Just how does a muscle grow bigger and stronger?" He explained that you must bring the muscle to a position of exhaustion and then, when you believe in your heart that you have nothing left to give, take it just a little farther. As a result, microfibres tear in the muscle; with rest, they grow back bigger and stronger. Year after year, we see the same people in the same condition because they exercise just enough to maintain their present shape. They do not take their training to the edge.

Developing mental toughness is similar. We must make a conscious decision to spend focussed energy exhausting the mental muscles that we want to see grow, strengthen and improve.

Some claim that they lack the personality to be mentally tough. Unfortunately, most people have the mistaken idea that mental toughness must be present from birth. While it may be true that some of us grow larger muscles more easily than others, each of us can substantially improve our muscle mass through recognition, desire and effort. Developing mental toughness has the same growth curve. We must recognize our need, want to improve, and focus our efforts toward the desired result.

Once we recognize the need to begin the battle for our minds, we can then welcome the positive, and consciously discard any destructive thoughts. We have taken the first step towards developing the mental toughness that we need to help us compete.

Developing correct habits of thought is probably the precursor to most success. The writer and motivational speaker Og Mandino said, "In truth, the only difference between those who have failed and those who have succeeded, lies in the difference of their habits.

Good habits are the key to success. Bad habits are the unlocked door to failure." Substantial *change* in our attitudes and actions will happen as we choose to develop good habits of thought.

As author James Lane Allen put it, "You are today where your thoughts have brought you; you will be tomorrow where your thoughts take you."

Golf legend Bobby Jones said it this way: "Golf is a game that is played on a five-inch course—the distance between your ears."

Dr. Seymour Epstein, when chair of the Psychology Department of the University of Massachusetts, confirmed these statements in his study of 50 "super-achievers." Over 10 years, he found the following nine basic similarities in the way these super-achievers chose to think.

1 Successful people are less sensitive to disapproval and rejection. This doesn't mean they don't care, it just means they don't carry the baggage of what others think around with them.

Successful people learn early not to worry very much about what others say about them. They embrace change, even though it is sometimes awkward for the rest of the world. Success often comes from setting a different course or doing what most people have never thought of. History is full of examples:

- The first steamboat took 32 hours to go from New York City to Albany, New York. People laughed.
- A horse and buggy passed an early-model car. People laughed.
- The first electric light bulb was so dim they had to use a gas lamp to supplement it. People laughed.
- The first flight lasted 59 seconds. People laughed.

Pavel Bure was one of the most exciting players in the NHL. It was my pleasure to play with him for a couple of seasons when he first joined the league. We both played for the Vancouver Canucks at the time, and everyone knew instantly that Bure was going to be a star.

Bure told me the story of his first 60-goal season in Vancouver. That season, hockey fans in Vancouver and around the league "worshipped him." However, 10 days into the post-season playoffs, after playing six games in the first round, Bure had yet to score a goal. Because of his 60-goal season, the expectations for Bure's performance were very high. During games 5 and 6, people actually booed him! The fans' opinion of Bure went from adoration to disgust to adoration again, as Bure went on to score the winning goal in overtime in game 7, moving the Canucks into the second round of the playoffs. Suddenly, everyone was back on the Bure bandwagon.

A professional athlete must learn not to embark on the emotional roller-coaster ride that the fans tend to be on and to refuse to worry about disapproval or rejection. I learned this lesson the hard way in 1982. I was traded from Washington to Montreal, and the corresponding headlines in the Montreal *Gazette* boldly proclaimed, "Worst Trade in NHL History." I clearly remember the pressure I felt to be superhuman in order to prove that headline wrong. I was being publicly disapproved of but was determined to make everyone say, "See, Walter proved them wrong; his play is incredible."

I internalized this disapproval until it made me ineffective. In one exhibition game during training camp, I remember being on a breakaway in the old Montreal Forum. I pretty much stickhandled into the corner, and I never did get a shot on goal. I wore that headline on my shoulders until we won the Stanley Cup in '86. I learned in Montreal—the mecca of hockey—to be far less sensitive to disapproval. We had a saying that I repeated often during my nine seasons with the Canadiens: "You're never as bad as they say you are, and you're never as good as they build you up to be."

Hockey players in Montreal have learned to deal with demanding fans. As a hockey dynasty the Canadiens organization has won 24 championships. When we were fortunate enough to work our way to the Stanley Cup finals in 1989 and then lost to the Calgary Flames in six games, the city of Montreal was in shock and went into a period of mourning. Other cities would have thrown a parade just for arriving in the finals. Not Montreal! The expectations were high.

I learned a lot about fans, and people in general, in Montreal. Another of our favourite sayings was, "The fans, they love you win or tie." Experience tends to desensitize us to disapproval and rejection, and this is a good thing. We need to worry less about what other people think or say and concern ourselves more with developing the internal character and mental toughness that will, in the long run, enhance our performance.

2 Successful people think bottom line. First they want to know who won, then they will have time to view the highlights.

Bob Gainey was one of the best leaders that I played with. Gainey had a way to get to the issue, to think bottom line. I remember Bob during a particularly important game gathering the bottom-line sense that our team was in a funk. The bench was quiet, our play was lethargic and Gainey perceived that something dramatic had to happen to shock us out of this mode of complacency. The players on the bench couldn't believe their eyes: During his next shift, Gainey went right after the toughest player on the other team and challenged him to fight. Bob very seldom fought and usually only in defence of a teammate, but he was sending a wake-up message to wake us up! Bob Gainey had an innate reading of the bottom line and what had to be done to improve it.

Over the years I came to understand the wisdom of the Montreal Canadiens' playoff philosophy of keeping players in a hotel even when we were playing home games. After winning or losing a critical game, every player scanned the game scores around the league and then as we gathered around a post-game dinner, there was time to watch highlights. This was, in fact, the process that created the bottom line.

3 Successful people focus on the task at hand. You cannot sidetrack super-achievers—they are consumed with what they are thinking about.

Two important principles collide here: "People get what they expect," and "People get what they focus on." Jacques Lemaire was one of my favourite NHL coaches. I experienced a difficult scoring drought as a player under Lemaire, and after a while he spent some time helping me out. He placed our backup goalie in net, me at the blue line, and then Lemaire took a bunch of pucks into the corner. He asked me to skate hard down the boards, then he passed me a puck, and as I approached the net for a shot he shouted, "Stop!"

"Ryan, what do you see?" asked Lemaire. I looked hard at the net from my position and said, "That's the problem, Jacques. I only see goalie."

Lemaire took me through this motion a number of times, always asking, "What do you see?" and always hearing the same reply.

Then Lemaire suggested a slight change. He told me that earlier video of my play indicated that when I saw only "goalie" at times in the past, I moved laterally across the net until I "found net." Wow, so simple yet so profound. With that small adjustment to my game and my confidence, I regained my scoring touch and went on to have a banner offensive year. In the end we get what we constantly focus on. Had I continued to only focus on shooting at the goalie instead of finding ways to focus on net, my success would have been limited. Focussing on the task at hand and the correct tasks over the long haul creates our desired success.

4 Successful people are not superstitious.

If something happens, it is not necessarily an omen. It is a waste of mental energy to believe that superstition has a connection to your performance. I played with many hockey players who believed that if they tied their left skate before their right skate and had a successful game, they had to use the same routine the next game in order to be successful again. Developing a mental routine can be helpful, but attributing your performance to superstitious habits is totally detrimental. The main reason that relying on superstition is unproductive is because it takes our focus off making the changes needed to succeed and sometimes keeps our focus on certain actions that have little or no connection to creating the outcomes that we desire.

5 Successful people refuse to equate failure with self-worth. When they do make mistakes, they will easily rebound and put the mistakes behind them.

Pat Quinn was our coach during my two seasons with the Vancouver Canucks. Pat has a great way of mixing the wonderful world of sports with real life. He made an impact on my hockey career and on my life. On the wall of his office was a plaque with these words: "A failed project is not a failed person." Successful people have learned not to personalize failure.

6 Successful people don't restrict their thinking to established rigid patterns. They don't think traditionally, but are highly optional.

In the early '80s, Jacques Lemaire was the coach of the Montreal Canadiens. These were learning years for me, and I loved every minute of the process. In Habs lingo, I was "learning how to *win*." Jacques Lemaire was a thinking player's coach. I loved playing the game of hockey; I loved being a professional athlete; but what I really loved was learning how to *win*. The Montreal Canadiens have, over the years, been able to pass down through their players and coaches a winning heritage. I was all ears.

As with so much of life, winning comes down to the little things. In the early '80s, our team was locked in a first-round battle of the Stanley Cup playoffs with the Boston Bruins. Boston had a terrific power play, and we clearly understood that for the Canadiens to be successful against the Bruins, we would have to neutralize it.

Ray Bourque was the main cog in the Bruins' power-play wheel. During the series, we came to realize that Boston was very good at gaining possession of the puck in our end. We knew that Bourque typically carried the puck to the red line and then took a full slapshot around the boards behind our net, where four other Bruin players would then head. Outnumbering us along the boards, the Bruins would gain possession and often get a good scoring chance.

We decided to be highly optional, to not restrict our thinking to the way we had traditionally killed off penalties. We realized that if we forced Ray Bourque to skate out from behind his own net a certain way, then he would be forced to dump the puck into our zone on his backhand or with a weak wrist shot instead of his powerful slapshot. We also sent one of our defencemen back into our zone more quickly. When Ray was forced onto his backhand, we had less trouble with the Bruins' power play.

Jacques Lemaire taught us to question how and why we did things on the ice. He taught us to not just play the way we had always been taught to play, but to play the way that created *wins!*

7 Successful people see the big picture.

Some rookies in the NHL play for today and do not prepare for a long career. Many young players arrive at the NHL level and believe they have fulfilled their dream: to *play* in the NHL. The bigger picture is for the young player to ready himself mentally and physically to *stay* in the NHL.

8 Successful people welcome challenges with optimism.

Apparently, the singer Willie Nelson bought his own golf course. Someone once asked him what was par on a particular hole. He answered, "Well, as a matter of fact, that hole over there is a par 47, and yesterday I birdied it."

During every turn in my 15-season NHL career, I found challenges hiding where I could never have imagined. These challenges were probably most apparent to me when injury struck. In December 1985, while playing at the Montreal Forum against our arch-rival, the Quebec Nordiques, I was accidentally struck in the eye with the blade of my opponent's hockey stick while he was following through on a shot. When I could not even detect the light shining in my eye from the doctor's flashlight, he knew that this injury could have permanent consequences.

During those long days of hospital rest (that is, don't move!) leading up to Christmas, I hit a turning point in my career and life. Maybe it was the cards that poured in from fans all over the country assuring me that they were praying for me daily; maybe it was the visits from my pregnant wife and our 18-month-old son, Ben, who couldn't fail to lift anyone's spirits; maybe it was my slow hockey player's brain finally recognizing that spending inordinate amounts of energy being upset about the inappropriate timing of injuries was only going to slow the healing process. Whatever the reason, this experience taught me to accept that stuff happens in life that is out of my control. Having an optimistic attitude, however, is totally in my control, and I recognized that I needed to spend less energy worrying and focus (no pun intended) instead on a positive recovery. When the doctors removed my patch, I could see again, and I continued playing through the early '90s.

9 Successful people don't waste their time with unproductive thinking.

Unproductive thoughts will cause us to lose sight of our goals.

My wife, Jennifer, and I developed a friendship with a young lady during our years in Montreal. Jennifer befriended her a little bit as a counsellor would a drug addict, because that was exactly what our new friend was. She was hooked on heroin. She would often say to us, "I want to be in love like you guys. I want to have the marriage and family that you both have."

My response, at least in my mind and to my wife, was, "Okay, you can have all of this if you first make the choice to get off the drug that is taking away your chance for life."

I can remember my wife and I responding to one of this woman's cries for help. It was quite a sad situation, really, but it had its humorous side. There we were, wandering around the seediest part of Montreal, trying to find her place so that we could help her evict another addict who refused to leave her apartment. We finally found her, and we decided to call the police to assist us. I'll never forget the look of utter surprise on the face of that policeman when one of the Montreal Canadiens answered the door. At least I had been wise enough to take my wife along, so it didn't look too bad!

We tried our best to help. We encouraged her to attend a highly successful recovery home in the mountains of New Hampshire called His Mansion, where she could learn the skills to get off heroin and get on with her life. At first she accepted this offer and was excited about the new direction her life might take, but then she changed her mind. She succumbed to her unproductive and destructive thoughts: "This is going to be too hard. I can't go off heroin cold turkey. New Hampshire is too far away." These destructive thoughts caused her to lose sight of her dream for a productive life.

We have since happily learned that she overcame her addiction in another way, but we were very discouraged with her choice at the time. Mental toughness is all about deciding what we are going to think about. We must seize control of our unproductive thinking and *stop, change direction* and *change* our *minds*!

It is fascinating to read the legendary stories about the Great Houdini. Although a masterful magician, Harry Houdini was probably even better as a locksmith. He had a standing challenge that he could get out of any locked jail in 60 minutes, provided he could enter in his regular street clothes and no one would watch him work. A town in Britain decided to challenge (and perhaps embarrass) the Great Houdini. This town had just built an escape-proof jail and invited Houdini to see whether he could break out.

Houdini accepted the challenge. He entered the jail in his street clothes, and the locksmith closed the door. With the clang of steel, everyone turned and left Houdini alone to work. He had hidden a long, flexible steel rod in his belt, which he used to try to trip the lock. He worked for 30 minutes, keeping his ear close to the lock; 45 minutes, and then an hour passed. He was perspiring. Finally, he was exhausted. He leaned against the door, and to his amazement, it fell open. They had not locked the door! The door was locked only in Houdini's mind!

How many times do we miss opportunities because we are locked into unsuccessful thinking? I have watched many professional hockey players complain publicly, "I am playing poorly, I just can't seem to score any goals, and I hope that I don't get traded." If an athlete is making these negative statements to the public, imagine what is going on in his or her mind. In effect, we talk ourselves into our goal-scoring slumps.

There is an old parable about a foolish peasant who was sent to visit his master's house. The master took him into his study and offered him some soup. As the peasant was about to drink the soup, he noticed a small snake in his bowl. Not wanting to offend his master, he drank anyway, and within a few days he fell so ill that he was taken back to the house.

The master again led him into his study, where he prepared some medicine in a small bowl and gave it to him. Just as the peasant was about to drink the medicine, he noticed another snake in the bowl. This time he pointed it out, and he loudly complained that this was the reason he had become sick in the first place. Roaring with laughter, the master pointed to the ceiling, where a large bow was hanging. "It is the reflection of the bow blowing in the wind you are seeing," he said. "There is no snake at all."

The peasant looked again and, sure enough, there was no snake in his bowl, only a reflection. He left the house without taking the medicine and regained his health within the day.

When we put limitations on ourselves, we have swallowed imaginary snakes. And they are always real ... until we find out otherwise.

The possibilities of thought-training are infinite, its consequences eternal, and yet few take the pains to direct their thinking into channels that will do them good, but instead leave all to chance.

—Brice Marden, American abstract painter

Physical preparation to play at the NHL level requires amazing dedication. In fact, today's NHL player is in better shape than players were in previous generations. I recognized early in my NHL career that physical preparation was extremely important, but I also found that if I developed my mental toughness, I would gain a significant edge over players who played hard only when they felt like it. While I was playing professional hockey through two decades, I worked to focus my reading and research on the exact areas that I needed to improve. One of the best compliments that a player can receive from his peers in the game of hockey is, "He comes to play every night." By working on my "mental muscles," I was ready to play my best, whether I felt like it or not.

Over many years of involvement in professional sports, I have found that mentally tough people excel in the following four areas:

1 Mental rehearsal: viewing a desired action in your mind's eye increases real-time execution.

Abe Pollin was the owner of the Washington Capitals during my first four years in the NHL. He and his management team had drafted me early in the first round of the 1978 NHL entry draft, and they made me team captain in my second season with the Caps. A few years ago I spoke with Pollin in a phone call that happened to coincide with an important event in his life. He was to speak to 800 people that evening, while accepting the Entrepreneur of the Year Award at a posh hotel in Washington, D.C.

Pollin told me the story that he intended to share with his audience that night. As a 16-year-old in high school, he had been a pretty good athlete. He wanted to try out for the high school basketball team, but at the last minute he "chickened out" because he was afraid of being cut! That whole season he watched every game from the stands, knowing that he could have been there.

Pollin told me he decided at that moment that he would never again let the fear of failure stop him from trying. "I promised myself that I would never sit on the sidelines watching other people go ahead and do what I could have been doing."

"In my life, Ryan," he added, "51 percent of the time things have turned out all right. I have failed at the other 49 percent of the ventures that I have tried, and some of those failures have really stung."

At the time, he had just sold his portion of the Washington Capitals and a portion of the Washington Wizards for 85 million dollars! The point that Abe Pollin and I talked about on the phone that day was simply this: you miss 100 percent of the shots that you do not take.

Imagine Abe Pollin as a 16-year-old, just before he was about to try out for the high-school basketball team. He allowed his mind to rehearse his not making the team! He made the suggestion to his subconscious mind that "maybe you shouldn't be doing this. You may get cut, so why bother trying?" This has happened to everyone at some point. We allow the mental rehearsal of the possibility of failure to overpower our ambition to accomplish a goal in an area in which we are likely to succeed.

A study of the application of mental rehearsal was done with basketball teams. One group practised shooting baskets on the court. A second group did nothing at all. A third sat silently in a room and, with closed eyes, imagined shooting baskets. As expected, when tested later, the team that physically shot baskets outperformed the team that did nothing. The surprise came in the discovery that the team that only mentally rehearsed the motion of shooting actually performed as well as the team that physically rehearsed the action.

Successful people stop themselves when their minds begin to rehearse failure. They reprogram their minds to rehearse the actions or attitudes that will bring success. Rehearse successful outcomes, and then step up to the line. Remember, we miss 100 percent of the shots that we do not take!

2 Mental expectation: create the win in your mind's eye.

During the 1999 World Championships of hockey, Canada and the Czech Republic were tied at the end of regulation play. Under the tournament format, the two teams would next compete in a shootout to decide the winner of the game. The shootout consisted of five players from one team moving in from the red line one at a time, trying to score on the other team's goalie. The opposing team would also get their shots and the team with the most goals would then win the game.

The two teams involved had very different attitudes toward the impending shootout and expressed these views publicly. Team Canada goaltender Ron Tugnutt told the *Vancouver Sun*, "The thought of a shootout had been going through my mind for the last five days. My worst nightmare had come true."

Conversely, Radek Dvorak of the Czech Republic team told the *Sun* he had been looking forward to the shootout. "We wanted to go to penalty shots, because it is our best chance. We can score goals on penalty shots; many guys can."

Can you guess the outcome? The Czech Republic won the shootout and enjoyed every minute of it. Winning mental expectations are crucial to a winning performance.

A while ago, I met Olympic and two-time world shooting champion Lanny Bassham. Bassham believes that 95 percent of all winning is done by 5 percent of the participants. He studies the mechanics of mental training and wrote an excellent book entitled *With Winning in Mind.* In it, Bassham tells the story of meeting Darrell Pace while competing in the 1976 Summer Olympic Games in Montreal.

Pace competed in archery that year at the age of 19. He stood 5 feet 10 inches tall and weighed 110 pounds. Bassham was amazed at Pace's attitude of sheer confidence. He referred to the gold medal he wanted to win in his event as "my medal." "Everyone is after my medal, but they cannot take it away from me." In essence, Darrell Pace had already won the gold medal in archery many times over in his mind. This was not cockiness. When asked why he was so certain that he would win, he responded, "Because I am more committed to mental training than any of my competitors."

 Dream lofty dreams, and as you dream, so you shall become. Your vision is the promise of what you shall one day be; your ideal is the prophecy of what you shall at last unveil.

—Denis Waitley, *Seeds of Greatness: The Ten Best-Kept Secrets of Total Success*

During daily preparation for the 1999 AFC Championship game of the National Football League, Tennessee Titans coach Jeff Fisher had his team practise the types of plays that they would need to be successful during their weekend game. He also had his team practise receiving the AFC Championship trophy. Each day, when Fisher gave the signal, the team not only imagined themselves receiving the trophy, they actually acted out the scene! When the Titans won the AFC Championship and gained entry into the Super Bowl, they received the trophy just as they had practised all week.

I learned this by my experiments; that if one advances confidently in the direction of his dreams and endeavours to live the life which he imagined, he will meet with a success unexpected in common hours.

— Henry David Thoreau, American essayist

Success flows to people who have great expectations. Many professional athletes are satisfied with just making a living playing the game they enjoy. Other players develop an early expectation to win a championship. One thing is certain: If players never develop a deep desire and expectation to accomplish, they never will. Expect it.

Rarely will you ever accomplish more than you expect to accomplish. So get in the habit of expecting the best. Your expectations by themselves do not create your reality, but they do indeed set its direction.

What do you expect to achieve today, this week, or this month? How do you expect other people to relate to you? Expectations guide our actions. When we know what is expected it gives us a clear plan of exactly what to do.

Whatever you sincerely expect, you will work for, you will nurture, you will persist for, and give power to. Those things will serve to make it happen. Expectations powerfully influence both your conscious and subconscious actions.

If you expect the day to be dreary and boring, most likely it will be. When you expect the day to be productive and fulfilling, you'll find yourself acting to satisfy those expectations. Make it a point to expect the best and then commit to following those expectations.

—Ralph Marston, American marketer and writer

3 Mental vision: discipline your mind to see opportunities rather than obstacles.

In his book *Learned Optimism*, Martin Seligman found that 75 percent of all people who go into the insurance business drop out within three years because of the high rate of refusal. Seligman asked the president of Met Life to hire the people who had failed their initial insurance test but passed Seligman's optimism test. These people outsold established insurance sales people already in the business by 21 percent in their first year. At the end of the second year, they outsold them by 57 percent. Disciplining our minds to see opportunity regardless of the circumstances and choosing an optimistic mindset are precursors to success.

 Obstacles cannot crush me. Every obstacle yields to stern resolve.

—Leonardo da Vinci, Italian painter and inventor

Gail Devers was training to compete at the 1992 Barcelona Olympics when sores suddenly broke out all over her body. No one seemed to know what it was. Finally she was diagnosed with Graves' Disease, a condition that had doctors threatening to amputate her feet. Eventually she began to improve. Overcoming this adversity, she went on to win the 100-metre race in Barcelona, and then, with a hometown crowd of 85,000 cheering her on, she repeated this amazing feat in Atlanta in 1996. "I wouldn't change a thing," said Gail, looking back on her ordeal. "It was a blessing. It made me the person I am today. It made me a stronger, better person."

As a 16-year-old, I had already moved away from home (with my parents' support and blessing) to pursue my dream to play in the NHL. That season, I was playing in Langley for the British Columbia Junior Hockey League. Our parent team in the Western

Hockey League was the Kamloops Chiefs, and during the playoffs they called me up to play.

Late in the game, I had the puck with good outside speed and was already around the defenceman heading to the net when I felt my feet go out from under me. The defenceman had swung his stick in desperation and knocked me out of control. I hit the net at high speed, and my knee made vicious contact with the goalpost. Back then the posts were anchored solidly into the ice.

My knee was a mess. I wore a cast from hip to toe for months, and when the doctor asked me to move my leg after he had cut away the cast, I couldn't. My leg had atrophied so severely that there was hardly any muscle to move it.

Rehabilitation began slowly and continued well into the next hockey season. I started poorly, skating with a large knee brace, and by Christmas my coach, Harvey Roy, was exasperated with my play. In front of our team, he gave me a verbal wake-up call suggesting that my backside better get in gear. My game jumped back on track.

In hindsight, I am able to say that the knee injury at 16 may have been a defining moment in my athletic career. Rehabilitation was harder than anything that I had experienced before. I learned how to handle significant amounts of pain as the therapists slowly broke the adhesions that had built up during the period of non-movement when I had been in the cast. All this work and pain showed me just how much it would take to compete, and just how much I really wanted it. It made me a tougher, more disciplined player. This difficult situation turned out to be an incredible opportunity for me, yet only hours after my knee operation the doctor had told my parents that the damage was severe enough that I would never play hockey again. In actuality, I played three more years in the Canadian Hockey League, was selected second overall in the 1978 NHL entry draft and went on to a 15-year career in the NHL.

I am thankful to the doctors for their wonderful work on my knee. I am also very grateful for the atmosphere of hard work and perseverance my family created, which encouraged me never to give up on my dreams. My parents' response to difficulties was invariably to work through them, not sit still and complain or philosophize. So I chose to look forward and went to work on strengthening my knee. I honestly don't remember dwelling on this situation much. I only remember working hard at rehab. The thought of not playing hockey ever again was never an option, because I *never allowed it to enter my mind!*

Many people allow their mental vision to be a deterrent to their opportunities for success. Those with an "I am a victim" mentality tend to whine about the situations they find themselves in, and because they continually put the blame on others they never find the power to change. Solution-driven thinkers are less concerned about what is happening to them and more concerned with their mental vision. Adapting and readjusting their mental vision allows solution-driven thinkers to overcome obstacles and move toward their goals.

 **There is no sadder sight than a young pessimist.**

—Mark Twain, American novelist and humorist

A pessimist sees difficulty in every opportunity; an optimist sees opportunity in every difficulty.

—Winston Churchill, British prime minister, statesman and author

4 Mental focus: focus your thoughts on present-day living and this-moment performance.

The great baseball pitcher Orel Hershiser was once asked how he pitched a near-perfect game in the World Series. Hershiser replied,

"I concentrate on one pitch, and then after that, one more pitch." Hershiser recognized that his success depended on breaking his performance into "bite-sized" pieces on which he could focus his mind. Perform in the present moment. Concentrate on the action that needs to be taken now, and ignore what happened yesterday or what needs to be done tomorrow. Mental toughness forces us to stay in the present. We cannot allow ourselves to hijack opportunities today by dwelling on the past or worrying about the future!

A study at Stanford University concluded that 58 minutes out of every hour are spent in the past or the future. The communications guru Marshall McLuhan used to say, "We are going 100 miles per hour down the road of life, with our eyes fixed on the rear-view mirror." Each time our thought process takes us back or forward, we must set parameters for what we allow ourselves to think. Is it constructive? While looking back at life, are we gaining valuable insights, or ruminating on negative things that are now beyond our control? Did I learn from that past experience? Will dwelling on it help me accomplish my present goals?

John Kehoe, in his book *Mind Power*, put it this way, "Your mind is a garden which can be cultivated or neglected, and you are the master gardener. You can cultivate this garden, or you can ignore it, and let it develop whatever way it will. But make no mistake—you reap the harvest of your work or your neglect."

In the words of Olympic track champion Jesse Owens, "There is something that can happen to every athlete, every human being—it's the instinct to slack off, to give in to the pain, to give less than your best—the instinct to hope to win through luck or your opponents' not doing their best, instead of going to the limit and past your limit, where *victory* is always found." Defeating those negative instincts that are out to defeat us is the difference between winning and losing, and we face that battle every day of our lives.

It is essential to replace negative, destructive thoughts. We can create fresh starts with quick beams of positive thinking. Dwell on what is good, wholesome and true. Do we have control of the things on which our minds dwell? If not, then who does? Is it the TV, radio or music we listen to that has the most influence on what we think? Is it our friends and what they say, or our coach and what he or she doesn't say? Simply allowing life to come at us, without controlling its influence on our thinking, will frustrate our desire to accomplish great things. If we really want to succeed, we must become the captain of our ship and take the helm of our "command control centre." We must first discipline our minds to think positive, constructive thoughts that will help us achieve our goals.

The essence of being mentally tough is to break through habitual thought patterns and their consequent actions by focussing our minds on doing what is right, rather than what is merely convenient. Developing mental toughness will allow us to gain mental control of our lives.

Collecting my thoughts on mental focus motivated me to "practise what I preach" in a specific area of my life. Jennifer and I have five wonderful children: two beautiful girls and three handsome boys. Just working through the evening's homework is enough of a challenge, but of course the busyness of our lives does not stop there.

Our three boys chose to play minor hockey (I know what you're thinking, but they really did have a choice!), and therefore our weekends from September to April were spent at the ice arena. Jennifer was involved in church and community activities. Add to that my schedule, including broadcasting 65 NHL games as a hockey analyst, my work as president and co-founder of Hothockey.com (an exciting venture combining my passion for hockey with the Internet), motivational-speaking engagements and, most important, coaching my sons.

The pace of our lives caught up with me in an unexpected way: I put on 20 pounds. As a professional athlete, I was motivated to put aside time daily for intense exercise and conditioning. When I retired from hockey my priorities changed, and gradually my time allotment toward exercise was replaced by the urgency of other matters. The major error, in retrospect, was that I kept eating at the professional athlete's consumption rate without expending the same type of energy.

I decided that a busy life is no excuse for unhealthy eating habits and lack of exercise. I recognized that I must refocus my mind. I decided to utilize mental toughness and apply these principles to this specific area of my life.

I decided that even though I continued to be busy, and obviously my exercise routine would not be what it used to be, I could enact change in my eating habits and exercise enough to be fit. There were times when I wanted sugar and dessert because I had built these habits of desire and they were hard to break. When these desires surfaced, I *stopped*, mentally focussed on my goal and reminded myself that my desire to be healthy and in shape was stronger than my desire for the type of food that would stop me from accomplishing this goal.

You'll never leave where you are until you decide where you'd rather be.

In his book *Performing Under Pressure*, Saul Miller says that we think 50,000 to 60,000 thoughts per day, and for most people, two-thirds of their thinking is negative.

Successful author and pastor Chuck Swindoll, in his *Insights for Living* radio series, asks us to "imagine that our minds are the *bank* and positive thoughts going into the bank are deposits. Unless we build positive deposits, we will never be in a position when we need it to have positive withdrawals." Swindoll goes on to make a significant point: "Don't forget that the *interest* that we accrue on our positive deposits is *joy!*"

One morning I was running late as I rushed out to my pickup truck to zoom off to the airport to catch my flight. Checking my pockets for my keys, I realized that I had accidentally locked them in the truck the night before. When you're late, these things seem to happen twice as often. Then I remembered that months before, I had prepared for times like this and stuck an extra key in a magnetic box under the chassis of my old truck. The box was there, the key was in it, the key opened the door, and I made the flight on time (barely). We need to discipline ourselves to make positive deposits when times are good. I made a positive deposit (storing an extra key for an emergency) when the time was good (I had lots of it), and it was waiting for me just when I needed it most.

While we are experiencing success, or even contentment, in any area of our lives, we need to pause and be consciously thankful, depositing a vivid, positive memory for future withdrawal. When times are tough or we're running on the edge, it will pay off in spades.

Developing mental toughness is a two-way, ongoing process, much like breathing. We exhale poor thought habits and inhale successful ones. As our mental toughness increases we are better able to adjust to change and challenge, whether it is starting a business, recovering from an illness or injury, rebounding from failure or competing for the Stanley Cup. Mental roadblocks can be negotiated and conquered when we are confident and mentally prepared. Life is like baseball, of which legendary baseball manager Yogi Berra famously said, "Ninety-five percent is mental, and the other half is physical."

Ryan in the broadcast booth with Jim Hughson.
(Photo by Jeff Vinnick/Vancouver Canucks)

Chapter 2 **Be a Communicator: Choose Successful Words**

No man means all he says, and yet very few say all they mean, for words are slippery and thought viscous.

—Henry Brooks Adams, American historian and writer

PAT BURNS BECAME OUR COACH in my last years with the team in Montreal. After we lost in the Stanley Cup final to the Calgary Flames, management decided to reduce the older players' ice time significantly in an effort to give the younger players more responsibility. During this time Pat decided not to play me in a playoff game in Boston Garden against the Bruins.

I had always taken great pride in helping our teams compete hard in Boston. In fact, I had come to love playing in the Garden. So, needless to say, I was very upset when Burns didn't dress me that evening. I knew I would have to deal with my response to this news. I decided to work hard to be a positive team player by encouraging our guys as much as possible at the right times, and the rest of the time staying out of their way.

We lost the game. I chatted briefly with Billy, a long-time friend and fan of mine from Boston, and then I headed to the team bus. I was the first person (other than the driver) to sit on the bus, and a little to my surprise Pat Burns was the second. Burns, in his rough-and-tumble way, stormed to the front seat of the bus and yelled out, "That's all I need, Wally!" At this point my brain was racing: my nickname on the team was Wally.

Burns' statement was puzzling. After trying to display a positive demeanour, rather than sulking about, for some unknown reason I was in trouble with my coach anyway. I began to reconstruct in my mind why he was upset with me, and I came up with a pretty logical scenario: "I'll bet that when Burns was walking to the bus, my friend Billy gave him an earful." Billy had told me after the game that Burns was crazy not to play me in Boston Garden, so I began to wonder whether Billy had perhaps said the same thing to Burns.

After a long ride to the airport, with me stewing over this situation the whole way, I decided that I must communicate and straighten out whatever had gone crooked between Burns and me. Once on the plane, I walked down the aisle to Burns' seat, leaned over and said, "Burnsy, is there anything that you're upset with me for?"

A puzzled look came over his face and he said, "No, Wally. Why?"

I replied, "When you jumped onto the bus at Boston Garden, you yelled out, 'That's all I need, Wally!'"

Pat chuckled. "It wasn't you!" he said. "Just as I reached the bus thinking how poor the refereeing had been, the supervisor of refereeing, Wally Harris, happened to walk by the bus, so I let him know what I thought."

In this situation, had I not communicated my perception of what was said, I would have been angry all summer, wondering why the person in direct control of my career was upset with me. I am always amazed at how easily misinformation can sink the ship.

In the world of professional sports, wrong perception is usually a product of unclear communication. And this is not a sports-only issue. In marriage, business, politics, parenting ... how many times throughout our lives do people get the wrong impression about what we say or do? Someone once said to me that he was more concerned about his internal character than the external world's perception of him. I appreciate this statement, but I have come to recognize the importance of managing both. Experienced communicators recognize the pitfalls of misperception.

THE COOKIE THIEF

A woman was waiting at an airport one night,
With several long hours before her flight.
She hunted for a book in the airport shop,
Bought a bag of cookies and found a place to drop.

She was engrossed in her book, but happened to see
That the man beside her, as bold as could be,
Grabbed a cookie or two from the bag in between,
Which she tried to ignore to avoid a scene.

She munched cookies, and watched the clock
As the gutsy cookie thief diminished her stock.
She was getting more irritated as the minutes ticked by,
Thinking, "If I wasn't so nice, I'd blacken his eye."

With each cookie she took, he took one too.
With only one left she wondered what he'd do.
With a smile on his face and a nervous laugh,
He took the last cookie and broke it in half.

He offered her half as he ate the other.
She snatched it from him and thought, "Oh brother,
This guy's got some nerve and he's also rude.
Why he didn't even show any gratitude."

She had never known when she had been so galled
And sighed with relief when her flight was called.
She gathered her belongings and headed to the gate,
Refusing to look back at the thieving ingrate.

She boarded the plane and sank in her seat,
Then sought her book, which was almost complete.
As she reached in her bag she gasped with surprise,
There was her bag of cookies in front of her eyes.

If mine are here, she moaned with despair,
Then the others were his and he tried to share.
Too late to apologize she realized with grief
That she was the rude one, the ingrate, the thief.

—Valerie Cox

The woman in this poem provides an example of the way many of us typically communicate—we don't! All that the lady had to do was ask the gentleman politely if that was his bag of cookies. I find that we need to communicate as early as possible. Had she asked the question as soon as the situation developed, her problems would have been solved before they grew worse. Never make the assumption that you have communicated. I have come to the point where I will ask the "silly question" to make sure that what I want to communicate has been received the way I intended.

I was invited to be the men's coordinator for a Billy Graham crusade scheduled for Montreal. At the last minute, Reverend Graham could not attend because of broken ribs. His brother-in-law, Leighton Ford, came to speak in his place.

During one of the services I attended, I was seated in the VIP section because of my work organizing the crusade. The lady next to me asked me where I lived, and we began chatting while music played in the background. I thought this woman said she was Leighton Ford's mother, and she had just arrived that day.

During Ford's presentation, I commented a number of times that her son was doing an excellent job. She asked me for an autograph, and I pulled out my hockey picture (I gave away plenty that night) and signed: "You must be very proud of your son. Ryan Walter." All was well, until Ford finished by thanking some important people in his life. He pointed to the lady next to me and said, "I am so pleased that Jean, my wife, could be with us this evening all the way from North Carolina."

I almost died. I had thought I heard her say that she was Ford's mother. When I later told my wife what I had done, she couldn't believe it. "Didn't you realize that she would have to look a lot older to be Leighton Ford's mother?" But I hadn't thought of that. Guys don't usually pay attention to these things.

Communication is not only what we say, but also how well we hear what is being said. Good communication skills reduce the chance that we will make fools of ourselves!

Many people prefer silence when it comes to resolving difficulty in relationships. Researchers at Case Western Reserve University in Cleveland discovered the brain-sapping effect of the silent treatment when they paired students with research team members and stuck each pair in a room for four minutes. They told half the students to ignore their partners and half to strike up a conversation.

Later, researchers gave each student 20 word puzzles to do. Those who had talked with their companions were more persistent in their efforts to solve the problems than those who had ignored their partners. "This suggests that consciously ignoring people requires a lot of mental energy," said study leader Kristin Sommer, now associate professor of psychology at Baruch College in New York City. "Talking is almost always the best approach," Dr. Sommer told *Prevention* magazine. "It's communication that solves problems, not silence." I took this approach with Leighton's wife and apologized at least 20 times. I felt brutal, but she was so gracious to the stupid hockey player. So I again say sorry to Jean, and I thank her for her incredible response to my inadvertent mistake.

Misperception of what was, or was not, communicated saps an athlete's energy and reduces his or her ability to perform. Prolonged silence over these misperceptions can lead to disaster. Teams, families and businesses all need to develop an environment where communication is encouraged.

Never make assumptions! Insist on clear communication. When in doubt, request, respond or reiterate. Former United States president Ronald Reagan used to tell a joke about making assumptions. Years ago in central California, a number of forest fires broke out simultaneously. A cameraman from a large daily newspaper was contacted by his editor and told to get to the local airport as soon as possible. "There will be a small plane waiting, and we need aerial photos of the biggest fire for tomorrow's paper." The cameraman hurried to the airport, eyed the closest plane with the engine running and hopped in.

After takeoff, the pilot turned to the cameraman and asked, "What should I do now?" The cameraman told him to head toward the largest fire. With an odd look on his face, the pilot asked, "Why would we want to do that?" The cameraman, now very confused, said, "I have to take photos of the fire. Didn't the paper tell you?" The young pilot's voice began to crack. "You mean, you're not the new flight instructor?"

I was once asked to punctuate the following sentence: Woman without her man is a savage. It could become, "Woman! Without her, man is a savage." Another option is, "Woman, without her man, is a savage." The key to communication is understanding that we will not all interpret things the same way. Each person is influenced by his or her background and preconceptions. We must be sure that our intention has been clearly understood, and that we have clearly understood the intentions of others.

SELF-TALK

Everything said in the world of the professional athlete can be broken into two parts: *self*-talk and *team*-talk. I want to make a differentiation here between the concept of self-talk and the thought process that we dealt with in Chapter 1. Thoughts are often uninitiated and non conversational, while self-talk happens when we initiate internal conversation with ourselves. Team-talk is the conversation between ourselves and others. The words, body language and nature of what we say significantly influence the atmosphere around us.

During my 25-plus seasons associated with the NHL, I have observed how habits of self-talk and team-talk have contributed to the rise and fall of many players. Interestingly, these two areas of communication are very much connected. Self-talk will either build up or destroy a person's confidence. As we use positive self-talk to build our confidence, we can then begin building up our *team* with the things that we say.

The way in which we think of ourselves has everything to do with how our world sees us and how we can see ourselves successfully acknowledged by that world.

—Arlene Raven, American art historian and writer

An athlete's self-talk is a pretty good indicator of his or her self-image and has a direct impact on performance. Without realizing it, a professional athlete feeds on a constant menu of positive or negative conversation. Developing internal habits of correct self-talk always precedes external success. I watched Mark Messier while I was the colour commentator for the Vancouver Canucks telecasts on CTV SportsNet. Early in the 1999–2000 season, I travelled with the Canucks to Florida games against the Florida Panthers and the Tampa Bay Lightning.

During an off day, the Canucks were practising at the National Car Rental Center in Sunrise, Florida, and after practice I spent a few minutes talking with Messier about a young Canuck player who had recently joined the club. I suggested to Messier that this player was endowed with considerable talent and stature and should make an impact on the team. Messier agreed with my assessment, but he then confirmed what I suspected. He said, "Yes, I think you're right, Ryan, but he will have to greatly improve his self-talk to reach his potential."

Self-talk is an area of our lives to which we typically pay very little attention. I can remember once reading a book on dreams in which the author suggested that the reader try to remember, upon waking, what his dreams had been during the night. I'm not sure if I am like the "average Joe" in this area, but I very seldom spend waking hours thinking about the many dreams that I must have had the night before. However, during the period of time when I focussed on remembering some of the sequences of my dreams, I found that it worked. I could easily recall all or some of the events from the previous night's dreams. The same is true for our self-talk! Until we spend energy focussing on the communication that we have with ourselves, we seldom realize that we can take conscious control of the content of that self-communication.

AREAS TO COACH IN OUR SELF-TALK

Disappointment. During sporting events, a player's emotional engine is revving at high speed, and reaction and overreaction are often working faster than logic. For some players, their desire to perform at a high level actually gets in the way of their performance. When a player misses a glorious opportunity to score with the net empty, a normal reaction can be, "I can't believe it! How could I do this? That might have been the only scoring chance I'll get tonight. Come on, you idiot! Wake up! I'm never going to score." Such negative self-talk begins the descent down the slippery slope that weakens self-confidence and, inevitably, performance. Confident goal scorers and consistent performers with years of professional experience feel the same initial disappointment when missing the empty net. However, these battle-tested scorers have learned over the years to focus on the present and the near future, leaving what's already happened behind them. They know that if they are getting scoring chances, they will soon score.

Confident players teach themselves to play the odds. Recognizing that players must develop scoring opportunities before the puck will go in for them, they create corresponding self-talk: "The good news is that I'm getting scoring chances. I've been in this situation before. With the next opportunities to score, I know that I will get one. Refocus, reload the gun, this next shot is going in!"

Auto-responders. When we make positive self-talk a habit, we begin to automatically respond to situations according to the positive words we have programmed into our minds.

During my time in Quebec with the Montreal Canadiens, I learned, in a very limited way, the French language (this is a good story for teenagers who would like to drop their language class at school). I had passed French in high school, but just barely, because growing up on the west coast of Canada, I thought there was little need for an extra language.

Later in life, when traded to Montreal, I spent thousands of dollars learning how to talk to the French Canadian people in their own language. "Comment ça va?" is the French equivalent of "How's it going?" Over the years, I noticed that a popular auto-responder to this question was, "Ça marche," which is roughly translated as,

"It's going." In other words, "It's going, and most of the time it's going nowhere."

Our auto-response communicator kicks in more often than we realize, and therefore we need to focus consciously on the words we have programmed into our minds through our patterns of self-talk. Dynamic people doing dynamic things in life program their auto-response system to utilize dynamic words. "Hey, how's it going?" will produce such answers as "Excellent." "Awesome." "Really well." "Extremely well, thanks." Many times throughout my life I have needed to reset my auto-responder in precisely this way. The power in this principle is very simple. Henry Ford said, "If you believe you can or you can't, you're right." When we talk, we talk ourselves into what we say!

Harvard University's Dr. Herbert Benson found that 30 percent of any drug's effectiveness stems from the placebo effect. Believing that the drug will work triggers the corresponding neuro-circuitry in the brain. Choosing thoughts that follow the circuit of optimism will trigger our auto-responder to respond positively regardless of the situation, which in turn reinforces our self-talk. We have created a circuit of positive internal confidence that is ready to branch out and influence others.

TEAM-TALK

Team-talk is what we articulate to our external world. In the end, all teams, good and bad, are what they are because of the players and coaches. Teams take action, focus energy and work together toward specific results. For 40 years, I have observed teams in sports, family life and business. On more than one occasion, I have found that talented teams are easily shipwrecked by the power of loose lips. Spoken words have the power to either build teams or destroy them.

SPOKEN WORDS

I have always enjoyed the banter and joking that naturally happen in a team situation, and I believe these are among the things that most retired athletes miss as they move on to other endeavours in life. What is said to a teammate's face very seldom rocks the boat. But like a wild Montana bushfire, what is said about a teammate behind his back isn't easily put right.

Successful people build successful teams by focussing on what their teammates do well, utilizing positive, affirming words. Only critique the performance or character of a person in private, face to face.

Team-talk that works encourages people publicly and critiques their performance privately. Over the years, I have noticed that players with poor self-esteem have a strong need to "put down" those around them. Somehow, if they can lower a teammate in another person's estimation, they feel better about themselves.

Let's be honest. We all have this tendency, and, at one time or another, we have all talked down a "teammate" when we should not have. This is why we must choose to apply the following principle, even though it doesn't always come naturally or easily: Build with words publicly. Critique with words privately.

For those of us who are married, what type of words do we use about our spouse when he or she is not in the room? Years ago, it was "in" for a guy to talk about his wife as "the old lady." We all tend to laugh and have fun with things that are said about others, but I have observed that dysfunctional families, businesses and teams begin heading downhill when they use what I call "lazy talk." It's easy to say bad things about the people closest to you. We all have faults and problems. Successful people build successful teams by choosing to build people up through affirming words.

WRITTEN WORDS

The influence of team-talk can be profoundly increased when read in print. In professional sports, young athletes learn to be selective with their words when talking to the press. If spoken words are hard to take back, printed words are impossible. It is easy to hide behind the phrase, "I was misquoted," but most of the time what will come out in print tomorrow is pretty close to what was said today. I have noticed that mature players do not skirt the questions posed to them. They answer each question with their own slant on the situation, and most of the time they slant toward the positive. Team builders are aware of this, and they think through their answers carefully before giving them.

The written word can positively affect team building. When coaches post slogans or quotes around the team's working and living environment, these have a great impact on the players. My wife and I have noticed this with our teenaged children. Posting a clipped article that says that students achieve higher marks if they get nine hours of sleep per night actually had a great effect in our home. Just when we think that what we are trying to communicate has no impact, we discover that it does. They just don't want us to know that it does!

This is true in all team environments. Immediate feedback from players about a quote posted on a dressing room wall is unusual, but over the long run, the positive written word helps to set the course and build the environment.

In the dressing room of the Montreal Canadiens hangs this excerpt from John McCrae's poem "In Flanders Fields": "To you from failing hands we throw / The torch, be yours to hold it high." These inspiring words typify the Montreal Canadiens, who, in

1986, held the record for the most team championships in all of professional sports.

One way that the written word has changed my life is right here in these pages where you and I are meeting. I have gleaned principles and passions from the words penned by successful people throughout history. In *Life is Tremendous,* Charles Jones says, "Our lives are shaped by the people closest to us, and the books we are reading." I am connected to a number of people who have made a lifelong habit of reading. After "Hey, how's it going?" my next question to these people is usually, "What have you been reading lately?" Build your team by recommending books that have helped to build you!

PREPARATION

A final thought on self-talk, team-talk and communication in general: success in all of these areas doesn't happen by chance. Many athletes entering a team situation tend to just spout off the first things that come to mind without planning. After completing my 15 NHL seasons, my professional life moved into the broadcasting arena. As a rookie broadcaster, I had to pay my dues. A portion of those dues was the gruelling travel schedule; I spent those early years visiting little towns across Canada, broadcasting junior hockey for TSN. But by far the largest portion of my dues was paid learning how to prepare properly for my telecasts. Scott Moore, the man who hired me for TSN and was my boss with SportsNet, mentored me in the area of on-air presentation. His constant advice to me is foundational for any person who wants to communicate well:

- Continually find current, relevant, compelling content (be on the alert for material you can use later).

- Create a content-delivery system for storage and presentation.

- Present the content with concise, short statements, loaded with information and applicable stories.

- Deliver the information with authority, sprinkled with stories and humour.

Whether we are colour analysts for hockey games, coaches talking to their teams or executives addressing company investors, relevant information needs to be shared with as few words as possible. These words can only be delivered well if they have been well prepared. My game-day preparation far exceeds my on-camera broadcast, both in time and effort invested. The old days where the coach would walk into the dressing room and scream, "We played awful last night, we better play better tonight!" are over. So are the one-hour meetings with the team. Attention spans are shrinking, the need to communicate visually is increasing, and with the Information Age a new sense of content-expectation is developing. More players than ever are asking "why?" This generation cares less about a person's credentials and more about the messenger's content and delivery. Effective communication is well prepared.

Picture this: Two guys are driving down a gravel road. Ahead, they see a car swerving all over the place and kicking up dust. One man in the car says, "Crazy woman driver." His buddy laughs in agreement.

As the swerving car gets closer, their suspicions are confirmed; it is indeed a woman driver, who is now stopped on the road. The male driver rolls down his window and slows the car so he can give this woman a piece of his mind. She sees his head hanging out of the window and begins to roll her window down as well. As the man pulls up next to her car, she yells, "PIGS!"

The male driver is caught so off guard by such a rude comment that he forgets to give her a piece of his mind. In disgust, he stomps on the gas, kicking up gravel and rocks. As he flies around the bend, he runs into a herd of pigs walking across the road and rolls his car into the ditch.

The two men were not prepared to receive important information, because they were heavily influenced by their preconceived stereotype of a woman driver and spent their energy talking her down. The woman definitely didn't deliver enough content in her stressed-out state, despite her good intentions. This is a classic example of two-way miscommunication, and the results are typically disastrous. Let's prepare for success by avoiding misperception, by practising positive self-talk and by sharing clear and uplifting team-talk. By being proactive in our communication, we will reap huge dividends and keep ourselves out of a big pile of pig manure.

Ryan in his first meeting with one of his hockey heroes, Bobby Orr.

Chapter 3 **Be Focussed: Choose Successful Vision**

The majority see the obstacles, the few see the objectives; history records the success of the latter, while oblivion is the reward of the former.

—Alfred Armand Montapert, American industrialist and author

DURING THE 1980s, while playing for the Montreal Canadiens, I had two shots at winning the Stanley Cup. Though we lost to the Calgary Flames in 1989, we beat that same team three years earlier in 1986. Throughout these NHL seasons, the Montreal Canadiens were blessed with many players who had great leadership skills. The cream of the crop was Bob Gainey. Gainey was a deliberate yet gentle man. He communicated well in the dressing room and had a great sense of what was needed to keep the train moving in the right direction.

It hardly looked as if it were moving in any direction at all by the end of the 1986 season. We were in a dogfight to even make the playoffs. The high-flying Edmonton Oilers led the league with 119 points, had three players among the top 10 scoring leaders and were easily the favourites to win the Cup. We had talent—Mats Naslund had 110 points that season—but our team game was not on track. The confidence and intercommunication between players and coaching staff was strained. It became a season that players just wanted to see end.

Gainey recognized the severity of the situation and pulled some of the primary players together for a heart-to-heart meeting. Bob suggested that we decide as a group to do one of two things. The easiest direction to take would be to continue our uninspired play and internal bickering. This would probably result in getting the coach fired and some of our teammates traded by the end of the season.

The second option was much harder but more rewarding. We could choose to refocus—to get our eyes off all the things that we were complaining about and focus our vision on something much higher: the Stanley Cup. We would have to plug some relationship holes on our team and get our minds and bodies ready to compete at a very high level. Bob ended our talk by asking a poignant question: In the future, when we looked back on this season, did we want to see accomplishment or abandonment?

As a team, we began to pull together and were able to squeak into the playoffs. In the second round we beat the Hartford Whalers in seven games (the seventh was won in overtime) and began to pick up some positive momentum. We eliminated the New York Rangers next, and then met the Calgary Flames in the Stanley Cup final.

I had broken my right ankle with four games to go in regular-season play. After five weeks of rehabilitation and working out to stay in shape, I was able to put on both skates and play. I required an occasional shot to freeze out any remaining pain, but little details like that were not going to keep me from my dream of helping our team win the Stanley Cup. After the sixth game in Calgary, we flew back to a celebrating city with the Stanley Cup.

The core of our team had decided, two months earlier, to focus our energy toward team accomplishment. The choice we made was simple but had great impact. We chose to stop feeling sorry for ourselves, deal with our problems, pull together as a team and refocus on the very thing that everyone wanted. In sports, and in life, we all need to be reminded to take our focus off blaming others, to refocus our sight and energy toward improving our personal and team game.

CONTROL THE THINGS WE SEE

The exciting thing about our thoughts (Chapter 1), our talk (Chapter 2), our sight (this chapter) and our actions (Chapter 4) is that they are all areas of our lives that we can control. That's empowering! We need to control the things we think, say, see and do, rather than allow them to control us.

Focus has become a buzzword among professional athletes, and there are two important strategies to learn in this area. The first is to become able to shut out the inevitable distractions that take an athlete off his or her game. The second is to develop a state of focus that can be turned on and off as needed. The ability to concentrate on the task at hand is as valuable a skill in the athlete's tool box as physical talent or ability.

In my opinion, Tiger Woods and Wayne Gretzky share similar qualities of focus. As an 18-year-old playing junior hockey for the Seattle Breakers, I was named captain of Canada's world junior team, playing against the top 18- and 19-year-olds in the world. During the summer training camp, one player trying out for the team was a 16-year-old named Wayne Gretzky. We had all heard about Gretzky's scoring prowess, and I was immediately impressed with his ability, as well as with his personality and character. When the World Junior Championships ended after Christmas in 1977, Gretzky was the leading point scorer, not only for our team but also for the whole tournament. I spent the next 15 seasons in the NHL competing against Gretzky, while he played for the Edmonton Oilers and Los Angeles Kings, and the things that I admired most about him were his determination and focus.

Many people put Gretzky on such a high pedestal that they actually hoped to watch him fall. Gretzky, however, developed the ability that Tiger Woods talks about, keeping the "switch" on. There is a quote attributed to Gretzky that maybe helps put this into context: "The difference between a 5-goal scorer and a 50-goal scorer at the NHL level is that the 5-goal scorer can tell you the name on the goalie's pads. The 50-goal scorer is focussed on finding only net!"

A simple magnifying glass demonstrates just how powerful focus is. When I was young, we had the romp of the 30-acre bush right behind our house. Most days, after school, we would spend at least a portion of time there, depending on how long our street hockey game lasted. Knowing that young boys have a penchant for fire, my parents made sure I understood that I was not allowed to light matches in the bush.

Like many boys using their overly active minds, I rationalized my way around this request from my parents. With one little magnifying glass focussing the rays from the sun onto a piece of newspaper I could light a fire, and I wasn't using matches! At the time, I noticed something about this technique: the glass had to have just the right focus from the sun. To accomplish this task, one had to move the glass toward and away from the paper to find the perfect focus of energy to start the paper smoking.

Growing up in the Vancouver area, I played with and against many young hockey players who had more hockey talent and potential than I did. I went on to a long NHL career simply because I was able, at a young age, to focus my energies on rapid improvement as a player, and I was willing to pay the price.

Often in my NHL career, when heading into the post-season, an interesting thing happened. Several times management felt that our team needed to be sequestered in a hotel for the duration of the playoffs. On the day before a playoff home game, the team practice would be set for 4:00 p.m. After practice, the players and coaches would be bused to a local restaurant for some carbohydrate loading (I always liked that part), and after the meal our group was checked into a local hotel. Game day included the morning skate, the afternoon pre-game meal and a pre-game nap, and then we were bused to the arena for the home game. After the game the players were allowed to return to their homes. We'd start the whole thing over again the next day with the 4:00 p.m. practice.

The knock on this system of team preparation during the playoffs was that it was different from the regular-season routine, and it became a family sacrifice. However, the major benefit of this special playoff pattern was the way it built an increased atmosphere of focus. You can guess the topics of conversation at dinner the evening before the game. Hockey, hockey, and more hockey! I believe that this playoff routine helped to win games for us by giving us a strategic advantage in the area of focus.

Think about the success you desire, and strive to directly apply the following six steps:

1 Focus on where you want to land.

Broadcasting hockey games on television has been an enjoyable second career, with many similarities to playing in the National Hockey League. The preparation for a game is less physical yet just as demanding, and staying close to the people in this great game is a bonus.

One area of my life that has remained the same for the past 30 seasons is my travel schedule. I have always struggled with my time away from Jenn and our family—not because they can't cope without me, but because I miss them, and I have missed some milestones and important events in their lives. I have learned through these years to guard my attitude regarding travel (my job is a great way to pay the mortgage, and I am thankful for it) and see instead an opportunity to use my travelling time to read.

Another luxury of travel is connecting with the people sitting next to you. On one long flight to Calgary from Halifax, it was my good fortune to sit next to an airline pilot in transit to his next assignment. We shared pleasantries after I spilled coffee over both of us, and then I asked if I could borrow half an hour of his time.

For the next little bit, this pilot allowed me to fire questions at him about his profession. Flying a small plane was always on my top-five list of goals to achieve. As Jenn and I built our family of seven, flying had to move down the priority list, but my interest in the how-to side was still keen. I started asking technical questions about how to land and how to handle different problems. Then my pilot friend stopped me cold with this profound statement: "Ryan, you're missing a foundational step. A pilot should never take off unless he or she has a clear vision and flight plan of where they are going to land. All the rest of these technical how-tos come into play along the way, as you head the plane in the direction of the desired landing strip."

I pondered this statement for the rest of that flight, but in much broader terms. Many people get their planes moving in life but have no clear runway on which to focus, no clear visual goal in mind and nowhere to land their plane.

Stephen Covey, in his *Seven Habits* books, suggests that people start their life endeavours in the context of working backwards from how they wish to be eulogized at their own funeral. This future gaze allows us, through the busyness of executing our lives' flight plans, to keep our eyes on the place where we want to land. This is who I desire to be! This is what I desire to accomplish!

During my 30 years of flying, I am thankful that every airplane I have boarded has accomplished its crew's flight plan and goal of landing safely. These flights have not always been without major bumps and significant challenges. Circumstances may have dictated that certain flights did not immediately achieve their desired landing place, but after time, and with a different airplane, I have always reached my final destination.

Focussing on where we desire to land in our lives gives us a reason to take off. Many people never accomplish their dreams, because they are afraid to take off. Taking off in life requires an element of risk, but if we want to get somewhere, we must first launch. Focussing on where we desire to land gives each of us a firmer flight plan. If paying off the mortgage early is one target on our landing strip, then keeping this in our focus makes the decision of whether or not to buy a newer-model car easier to make.

When weather comes at us during our flight, we have to be flexible and manage our flight plan accordingly, while keeping our final destination in mind. It may even be helpful to write out short-, medium- and long-term goals weekly to keep the landing strip in focus.

Focus on where you want to land! We have to be able to see it before we can go after it and then accomplish it. If you don't know what you want, how will you know when you've got it? Some professional athletes I have known were focussed on the money. For most, however, money is not the goal, it's a by-product. Being the best we can be every game, improving, leading our teams and winning the Stanley Cup are the goals. If you accomplish all four of these goals in a season, then every team in the world will seek you out to give you more money than you can imagine.

The following four steps are the way of performance success:

- The goals and dreams shape our plan.
- The plan sets the action.
- The action achieves the result.
- The result brings success.

2 Focus on solutions.

As a professional athlete, I learned a number of important life skills. We looked at the importance of our habits of thinking in Chapter 1, and specifically at the fact that our conscious mind can only hold one major thought at a time. If we dwell on a positive thought, then the negative ones will have a much more difficult time reaching the forefront.

I have found through experience that we must replace a habitually negative thought with a positive one. In other words, it's not good enough just to say, "I'm going to stop doing that!" We must replace the action or thought that we are trying to remove with something much more constructive.

So it is with our focus. Most of the successful people I've come to know have developed the habit of looking hard for solutions. When tough times move in like clouds in a weather front, it seems to be human nature to react to the bad news in negative terms. It takes practice and hard work to find the breakthrough solution and then either fix the problem or leave it alone and instead fix our focus or attitude.

One of the most frustrating times during my 15 seasons in the NHL was 1990–91, my last with the Montreal Canadiens. Training camp that season took place in Moscow and St. Petersburg in Russia and Riga in Latvia. The effects of nearly a century of communism were still strongly felt, though the Soviet Union had recently dissolved, and the tension in the air was noticeable.

Jenn accompanied me, along with our three-month-old baby, Joey. I'll digress for a minute to tell my favourite story of the trip. Our team took some time for a tour of St. Petersburg, then still named Leningrad. This city was badly in need of restoration but still held spectacular architecture and culture. A young Russian student was our tour guide and interpreter for the day. At the end of our time together, he asked our team if we had any parting questions.

Well, you're beginning to know me a little bit through these pages, and you probably recognize by now that I am not very shy. I piped up with a question that had been on my mind since the beginning of the tour. I asked, "How much do you get paid for a day like today?"

The young student replied with a joke I learned later was often told to visitors, "Here's how it works in Russia: The government pretends to pay us, so we pretend to work." Wow, talk about telling it like it is!

During this season (my ninth as a Canadien, in my 13th NHL year) it was obvious that management was going with a younger core of players. From the beginning of training camp to the end of the exhibition schedule, right into the first week of the regular season, I hardly played. During each pre-game practice session, the group of players involved in the upcoming game conserved their energy and worked on the specifics of the game plan. The players not slated to play that night skated longer and harder, trying to maintain game shape. This was the first time in my career that I found myself "left out of the loop." My focus was really challenged, because our human nature tends to want to get mad and dwell on what a bad person the coach is. Through this time of career transition, I found myself gradually learning to concentrate on what I thought was the proper solution. As my focus finally moved off "poor me" and onto the things that I could control, I deliberately redirected my attitude toward my conditioning and helping the younger teammates with their game. This type of focus kept me upbeat, ready to jump in and play when I was needed.

If you are thinking, "Okay, Ryan, let's have the storybook ending. Your focus helped you get your game turned around, and you went on to score the winning goal in the last game of the Stanley Cup final." Wrong! Things actually got worse. The first game that I was in the lineup was against the Hartford Whalers. During my first shift on the ice, as the puck came to me in the neutral zone, I was hit from behind by a Hartford defenceman. I fell to the ice as I had thousands of times in the past, jumped up, skated myself back into position in our defensive end and received the puck again along the boards.

This time I moved through the neutral zone with the puck, sensing that something was wrong. As I went to shoot the puck into Hartford's end, my wrist flopped and the puck barely moved. Our bench was close to where I was positioned, so I headed there to Gaetan Lefebvre, our excellent trainer, to figure out what was wrong.

Lefebvre asked for the home team doctor to meet us in the dressing room. My wrist was now starting to swell, and we both understood that something was not as it should be. The Whalers' doctor thought I had only sprained my right wrist, but that statement was little comfort. Both Lefebvre and I thought it was much worse, and the X-rays proved us right. Dr. Eric Lenzner, our team surgeon, had to insert two pins in the three fractures the following day.

On the first shift of my first game back in the lineup, I had sustained a near season-ending injury! Now my focus was really challenged. During this time, I'll admit there were some down days of disappointment. I remember having to focus on the big picture as much as possible. In order to come out of this injury successfully and prolong my career in the game that I loved, my focus would now have to turn fully to conditioning and rehabilitation.

Looking back through the lens of the "big picture," I am pleased that with the help of Lefebvre, John Shipman (assistant trainer at the time) and my teammates, things worked out. I finished the season with the Canadiens and then went on to two very successful seasons with the Vancouver Canucks. My right wrist still has two pins in it, but it works just fine.

Focussing on finding solutions can be instantaneous or a long-term process. Either way, in order to focus on something, we usually need to first move our focus off something else. Complex emotional reactions to situations can cloud our ability to focus on the solution needed for today. Anger, bitterness, revenge and other destructive emotions need to be parked and replaced by focussing on a positive plan to move forward.

The emotion that tends to fog up our "focus glasses" the most is fear. Experience has shown me that the "fight or flight" fear response is an important God-given reaction, but it must be managed. Fear tends to move our focus toward what we cannot do, rather than keeping it firmly on what we want to do.

 Fear can be conquered. I became a better person and a better football player when I learned that lesson.

—Roger Craig, National Football League player

The Old Testament book of Numbers has an amazing example of what I call "debilitating focus." God had told the people of Israel to move to the Promised Land and live there. Moses sent 10 spies to bring back a report on the land and its inhabitants. The spies unanimously agreed that the land was fabulous, but they didn't agree on its "conquerability!"

Eight of the 10 spies focussed on the size and number of people inhabiting the Promised Land and convinced the people of Israel that the opposition was too great. This "fear report" sent this group of people wandering for 40 years in the wilderness, without even trying to take the land that had been promised them. Debilitating focus on fear ruined any chance of executing their game plan.

One of the best ways to appropriate the power of focus is to teach ourselves and our teammates to look past the fear in any equation and focus instead on what we want to accomplish. If our desire to accomplish a goal is strong enough, then there really is only one question: "How much am I willing to pay?" If we're willing to pay a high price to accomplish our goal, then fear will have no impact at all.

Most of life has a risk element to it. As Jenn and I take on situations of risk, we often start by focussing on what we envision could be the worst possible outcome. If we feel we can live with this, we move forward. Many times during my hockey career, I had to decide how high a price I was willing to pay to succeed.

In the late '70s, fighting was not only acceptable in the game of hockey but also, because of the Philadelphia Flyers' two Stanley Cup wins, it was actually in vogue. I employed this worst-case-scenario technique prior to games where I knew that I would be challenged to stand up and fight for my teammates. I would envision the worst possible outcome of getting into a scrap. Could I live with a black eye and a bruised ego? Sure I could. It wasn't about winning every fight in those days, it was about showing up, competing and not backing down.

Recognizing the worst-case scenario actually helped me look past my fear and gave me freedom. What had been, in the beginning, a debilitating focus on fear became an empowering resolve to play the game hard because I could live with whatever the end result happened to be.

An important point to make any time we discuss focussing on fear is this: most of what we fear about the future doesn't happen. As we discussed in Chapter 1, the Flyers' most powerful technique was their ability to change their opposition's focus from playing a successful game to fearing what "might" happen.

> **Conquering fear today allows each of us to face tomorrow's challenges head on, with the confidence of yesterday's success.**

If we are truly going to move forward, we must deal with our fear, and then learn to focus beyond it.

> If I were asked to give what I consider the single most useful bit of advice, it would be this: Expect trouble as an inevitable part of life. When it comes, hold your head high, look it squarely in the eye and say, "I will be bigger than you; you cannot defeat me."
>
> —Ann Landers, American advice columnist

One season, our two younger sons both attended a tryout for their respective Minor Hockey Association's rep teams. Most minor associations in hockey include a number of rep teams, and if children are not selected for that team, they then play in the association's "house league." I have coached our boys at both the rep and house levels, and from my point of view during the tryouts, I felt that both of should have made their respective rep teams, even though they didn't. Not being a pushy dad when it comes to our children's activities and sports, I kept my opinion entirely to myself.

Jenn and I talked during the tryouts about the attitude that we wanted to model for our boys during this situation. We hung our hats on a saying that I have developed over my years of competition: "Bumps in life (tough times or disappointments) force us down one of two roads at the intersection of Bitter and Better."

Each of us has observed people hit with similar circumstances. One person chooses to be bitter and focusses on life through the "poor me" set of binoculars. The other person chooses to get better and to work through the circumstance with a focus on equipping himself with new experience and new skills.

I articulated this "bitter or better" scenario to the boys, and we all decided to focus on preparing them for next year's rep tryout, while making the current season as much fun as it could possibly be.

3 Focus on developing the skill that gives you the win.

I do not know as much as I would like to know about the basketball coaching great, John Wooden. Under his tutelage, the UCLA basketball team won 10 national championships in 12 years—an amazing performance. I have learned some things about the Wooden philosophy through his writing and through articles written about him. The part that impresses me most about the John Wooden philosophy is the way he articulates his game plan through focus.

National Basketball Association Hall of Fame player Bill Walton, in his introduction to Wooden's book *Wooden: A Lifetime of Observations and Reflections On and Off the Court*, tells part of the story: "The skills he taught us on the court—teamwork, personal excellence, discipline, dedication, focus, organization, and leadership—are the same tools that you need in the real world. Coach showed us how these skills are transferable. He wasn't just teaching us about basketball, he was teaching us about life. John Wooden taught us to focus on one primary objective: Be the best you can be in whatever endeavour you undertake. Don't worry about the score. Don't worry about the image. Don't worry about the opponent. It sounds easy, but it's actually very difficult. Coach Wooden showed us how to accomplish it."

It is said that John Wooden never worried about winning. Instead, he focussed his energy and his team's energy on practising the details of their game that created the end result that he and his players desired. John Wooden is so right. Break down the game; understand what parts give or take away your success; practise these components, and during the game, if they are implemented properly, more often than not your team should win.

Great team performance comes when accumulative personal skill is combined with practised team execution.

As you might have guessed by now, I have always had great affection for the game of hockey. Since my mom introduced me to the world and my dad introduced me to the game of hockey, my love for this game has increased with every season. At 19 years old I was excited to play for the Washington Capitals in the NHL. Pieces of my dream were being lived out, and my hard work earlier in life was being rewarded. I learned early that making an NHL team was an honour and very difficult, but many players made it. That wasn't the really hard part. The most difficult thing for the NHL player to do is to develop the mindset that will allow him to stay at the NHL level. Many of my peers sustained their level of play to etch out long

NHL careers, but many more players came in for two years or two months and then never resurfaced.

During those early years as a Washington Capital I used to go to the arena a couple of hours early for practice and try to pick out an area of my game that I could consistently upgrade. At times, even professional athletes put in only enough time to maintain the status quo, but consistent goal scorers don't hope to score goals. They focus on practising the action that gives them the success. Players with sustained careers focus their practice time on improving all parts of their game with an emphasis on areas of need. Baseball great Pete Rose nails this one: "My father taught me that the only way you can make good at anything is to practise, then practise some more. It's easy to practise something you're good at, and that's what most people do. What's tough is to go out and work hard on things you don't do very well."

Paul Kariya, superstar player with the Nashville Predators, has developed an amazing aptitude for choosing an aspect of his game that is weak and then taking drastic action to improve it. When he was with the Mighty Ducks of Anaheim, Kariya decided he wanted to work on developing his backhand shot. The backhand has become a bit of a lost art for two reasons. The first is that the heel-to-toe curve in most blades takes away from the backhand shot's power; second, at the NHL level there is certainly less time and space to set it up. So Paul built some time and energy into his off-season to buy hours of ice time where he practised, among other parts of his game, the backhand shot. Paul Kariya may now possess the best backhand shot in the league. Even on the morning of the game, during pre-game practice I have seen Kariya with 50 pucks at the side of the net as he tuned up his backhand shot. By focussing on improving an area of his game that needed an upgrade, Kariya added another skill that allowed him to continue his dominance.

Golf's Arnold Palmer talks about the four Cs of playing better golf:

- Concentration
- Confidence
- Competitive edge
- Capacity for enjoyment

Concentration, or the ability to focus, is Number 1!

4 Focus on a superior set of skills that you want to emulate.

Roger Bannister was at one time the fastest human mile runner. Bannister first broke the four-minute-mile barrier in May 1954, but John Landry ran it even faster one month later. Bannister reclaimed the honour in August 1954 in a famous race here in my hometown of Vancouver. Some pundits in the world of sports believed achievement of the four minute mile to be impossible. Although breaking the barrier was an incredible feat, the important point is this: over the following 10 years, 336 runners achieved the same milestone. To excel in any area of life, the fastest elevator to the top is always populated with people who observe and apply the actions and attitudes of successful people who have gone before them!

An interesting case study for this principle took place during my 15-year NHL career. Goaltenders at this high level have always been pioneers. Styles change; first the stand-up goalie is hot, and then the "flopper" is in. The "butterfly" style of goaltending was not unique to Patrick Roy, but he brought this style to prominence.

It was my pleasure to see this rookie goaltender mature over the 1986 season to the point where he was nearly unbeatable during the Stanley Cup playoffs. Roy proved to be one of hockey's best goaltenders. His style was adopted in one form or another by almost every NHL goalie and by nearly 100 percent of netminders who grew up in Quebec, Roy's home province.

During my formative years, my father, Bill, was my hockey mentor. I watched him play the game at a recreational level and thought that I could never play as well as Dad. I grew up watching the styles of play of Gordie Howe, Bobby Orr, Bobby Clarke and Bryan Trottier.

During my post-hockey career in broadcasting, I looked up to Harry Neale with CBC's Hockey Night in Canada and to John Madden, a National Football League broadcaster. As a colour analyst, I could emulate the types of things these two men were doing and saying. I have been very fortunate to work with two of the best play-by-play men in the industry, Jim Robson and Jim Hughson; they have taught me every part of sportscasting—most importantly, their method of preparation and presentation.

Spiritually, I have had mentors. Socially, I have had mentors. In business, I have tried to shorten my own learning curve by asking people how they accomplished what I desire to accomplish.

As with most paths, there are a number of "watch-outs" as you move down this mentoring road. The most important, in my estimation, is to be careful to emulate the "success action," not the total person. I believe that God made each of us distinctly unique.

When I broke into the NHL (in the old days), in order to be one of the boys everyone would get together after practices or games for team building social times. We are all imperfect people, and I saw many things that players did and said that I did not want to emulate. They could show me ways of becoming a better hockey player, but I was certainly under no obligation to copy everything they did. When focussing on what your mentor can help you with, don't pick up the baggage. I can focus on and try to utilize the great traits of other people in my life without becoming them.

There are no shortcuts to the top, but following the path worn down by past successes lets us know that we are heading in the right direction.

5 Focus with heightened awareness of the end.

When I played in the NHL, there was nothing I liked better than playoff games that went into overtime. During the 1989 Stanley Cup playoffs with the Montreal Canadiens, the third game against the talented Calgary Flames was tied after regulation play. The teams were tied one game apiece in the series, and many people believed that Games 3 and 4 would be critical.

Both teams seemed to play tentatively through the first overtime period. Late in the second, well after midnight Eastern Standard Time, I was able to bang in a rebound off the initial shot by Stephane Richer. Our team went up two games to one. Then, during the crucial Game 4 and to their credit, Calgary came back to win in Montreal to make it two games to two and then went on to win Lord Stanley's Cup.

Personally, this may be my strongest regret in pro hockey. Had we really brought our best effort into Game 4, our team might have carried a 3–1 lead back into Calgary for Game 5. If we had truly focussed with a heightened awareness of the end, I believe that we would have won another Cup.

 If my doctor told me I had only six minutes to live, I wouldn't brood. I'd type a little faster.

—Isaac Asimov, American author and biochemist

Do you remember the *Seinfeld* episode where Jerry and George come up with the idea that the speed limit for driving should be indexed to age? When you're 80, the limit should be 80, because you don't have as much time left as a 65-year-old! The misconception about sudden-death overtime is that everyone runs around like panic-stricken chickens with their heads cut off, trying not to lose. Nothing could be farther from the truth. Successful teams develop players who understand how to participate in this type of pressure situation. Strategy and play execution remain very constant. Really, the only difference is this: in sudden-death overtime, players develop an increased focus because of a heightened awareness of the end.

Here's something I have been focussing on. All of us, at one point or another, will die. Why not develop the habit of living as if we are in sudden-death overtime? Prioritization of what's important seems to happen naturally when people prepare for death. There is a heightened focus on what needs to be accomplished. Without being morbid, people who want to be successful and fulfilled should live life in sudden-death overtime!

The game of football gives us a wonderful example of the possibilities of this principle. When a team needs points near the end of the half or the end of the game, the team with possession of the ball will often move into its "two-minute offence" routine. During this set-up, the team is three times more likely to score points than at any other time in the football game. Why? The same team is playing against the same opposition. Both teams are playing on the same field in the same atmosphere. What changed during the last two minutes that wasn't there during the other 58? The two-minute offence creates a heightened focus. Players recognize that in order to be successful, they must focus on where they want to go (the end zone) and the time constraint increases their motivation to get there.

While preparing to hit the ice in the game that would deliver the Stanley Cup to the Canadiens, a theme developed in our locker room. We began to talk about some of us never being in this position again. That fact created a heightened awareness, and this heightened awareness pushed us forward to accomplish our dream.

Many people well into their 80s and 90s, when reflecting on their lives, indicate that if they had another opportunity to live life over again they would change a few priorities. They talk about loving more (prioritizing relationships), risking more (not worrying so much about failure) and enjoying each day to the fullest. We can choose now to change our focus and live the life we should, instead of the life that might have been.

6 Focus on beating yesterday's performance.

Only with hindsight as my guide have I come to understand the importance of the principle of competing without comparing. Too many times, especially in professional sports, we get into the comparison game. Let's take my NHL career and compare it with Wayne Gretzky's. From the time we played together on Team Canada at the World Junior Championships during December 1977 and through to the end of our pro playing days, here's the picture: Gretzky scored 20 or more goals per season 15 times and 30 or more goals 13 times, while I had seven seasons with 20-plus goals and one with 30-plus. Gretzky finished his 20 NHL seasons with 1,487 games played, scoring 894 goals and 1,963 assists and amassing 2,857 total points. My NHL career lasted 15 seasons and 1,003 games, and I scored 264 goals, with total points at the 646 mark. Gretzky holds 56 NHL records and won four Stanley Cups. I don't hold an NHL record and have only one Stanley Cup ring.

I think you get my point. If I were to compare my statistical performance in the NHL with my peers, led by Wayne Gretzky, I might have reason for post-playing depression. But this isn't fair. We are different people, with different bents, different gifts and different lives to live. The important differentiation is: don't compare—compete!

While Gretzky was amassing these amazing statistics and breaking long-standing records, I competed against him, and our team competed against his team. Competition is invigorating and healthy. Comparison, however, is more about ego and propels us down a road that never ends.

The question to ask of those who live their lives comparing stats is, "When does it stop?" Do we compare the IQ of each other's kids? Do we compare the cars that we drive (I hope not, because I love my pickup truck), the vacations that we take and all the rest? It's been said that it is hard to save money when our neighbours keep buying things that we can't afford. In the comparison game, there is no end.

Concentrating on being better than yesterday gets our focus off what we cannot control (like Wayne Gretzky's talent) and on to the things we can control: our performance. Many times during the Summer and Winter Olympics, we hear comments from athletes such as, "This performance is my personal best. I was competing against a strong field and didn't accomplish my goal of winning a medal, but knowing that I performed my best time ever makes this trip worthwhile."

Making life's trip worthwhile comes by bettering our yesterdays! Focussing on being better than yesterday empowers our today and gives us hope for tomorrow.

Our business in life is not to get ahead of others, but to get ahead of ourselves —to break our own records, to outstrip our yesterdays by our todays, to do our work with more force than ever before!

—Stewart B. Johnson, British artist

Until we try to correct our focus, we may not realize that things were blurry in the first place. Focus on where you want to land, on solutions, on developing the skill that gives you the win, on a superior set of skills that you want to emulate, on your heightened awareness of the end and on beating yesterday's performance. Sharpening our focus in these six areas will guarantee strong results.

Ryan with his game face on: even late in his career, Ryan was willing to mix it up to help his team.

Chapter 4 **Be a Player:**
Choose Successful Action

The enjoyment of life would be instantly gone if you removed the
possibility of doing something.

—Chauncey Depew, U.S. senator

MOST PEOPLE AGREE that individuals can have almost anything
they want in life, if they are willing to pay the price to attain it.
After we build our confidence, attitudes and vision, we come to the
crossroads of connecting who we are with what we do. If we want
to excel at our vocation, one thing is certain: we must, eventually,
take action. To be accomplished in any field, most of us have to
dedicate hours, days, months and even years of practice to learn
and improve our set of skills. The author John Maxwell puts it well:
"Find something that you enjoy doing so much that you would do
it for free, and then work hard to develop skill in this area so that
other people will pay you to do it."

To be very good in any specific area, long periods of action will
be needed, so we'd better enjoy the action as we take it.

MAKE THE MASSIVE WORKLOAD NORMAL

I have seldom heard anyone express what I believe to be absolutely true: making the massive amounts of work required not only normal but also enjoyable is paramount to achieving success. During countless hockey seasons, I have been in more than 200 dressing rooms across North America. After one of our son's hockey games, I happened to remain in the dressing room for a while, and a parent of one of the boys came in to pick up the team jerseys, as it was her turn to wash them. Now, these were 15- and 16- year-old players, who have fully developed sweat glands. This mother yelled out, "Ooh, what an awful smell in this dressing room!" Her comment caught me completely off guard. For many years, I have spent good chunks of my life in hockey dressing rooms. I am as comfortable in the dressing room as I am in our family's living room, and in my opinion, there is no smell in a dressing room. I'm used to it! For most of us who have spent our lives close to sports, the smell is normal.

If you want to be good in sports, working out for three or four hours a day needs to be normal or routine, so why not enjoy it? Turn your "have tos" into "want tos," and all the action that you need to take to excel will be normal stuff. Imagine if your chosen endeavour demanded long periods of sustained action and you couldn't handle the smell of sweat. I'm afraid you're going to have to learn to like that smell!

Weekly routine for Canadian rower Gavin Hassett when he spoke to *The Vancouver Sun* about his preparation for the 2000 Summer Olympics: "A hundred and fifty kilometres of rowing per week; we lift a hundred-thousand pounds worth of weight per week. The Olympics are still eight months away, but we're training three times a day right now, in combinations of actual rowing practice, weight training and cross-training runs six times a week. We're quite busy but this is what it takes to get ready for the Olympics."

MORE ACTION FOLLOWS FIRST ACTION

When we want to maximize our action, we must improve our "first-mover advantage." The dot-com world has highlighted this phrase for companies like Yahoo! and Excite. These companies made many mistakes, but because they were able to come onto the Internet scene first in their category and gain market share, they have been successful. They exercised their first-mover advantage.

When taking action in any field, getting the jump on the marketplace helps build badly needed momentum. Prior to the 1981-82 season I spent extra energy preparing myself over the summer. It paid off. The first 10 games went very well for me offensively, and after seven games I was leading the NHL in scoring. The rest of the league's goal scorers then woke up, and I settled back in the pack. But thanks to the strong start, that season produced my best offensive numbers: 38 goals, 49 assists and 87 total points.

By the way, while I was Number 1 in scoring in the NHL, I also had a big black eye. You know what I did at this point? I proposed to my wife! Do you think I'm not a strategist? I knew the sympathy vote, combined with the celebrity status, would work in my favour! Jenn said yes, and I realize every day how blessed I am that she did.

When taking action in any area, it is essential to move quickly. Look to get first-mover advantage. Decide what you want to accomplish, then move into action right away to try to create the early success. So many goal scorers get one early in the first period of the hockey game and then go on to explode offensively. Early success after early action ignites early confidence and leads to a successful performance.

DON'T ACKNOWLEDGE THERE IS A SWITCH

Tiger Woods was asked if he would have trouble getting up for his next tournament after winning the previous one in a close playoff. Woods used an old Jack Nicklaus phrase when he told *Sports Illustrated,* "The switch is always turned on. There is no on/off switch when it comes to match play; if this week I'm competing in a PGA tournament, I am focussed on winning. The switch is on. Next week, if there is no tournament, I'm resting in preparation for the next one."

During my career in the National Hockey League, many players in countless dressing rooms have used similar words. "Come on, boys, let's get ready, the switch doesn't turn easily from off to on." I'd like to take the idea one step farther and get rid of the switch altogether. There is no possibility of switching anything off, because there is no switch. We are, simply, on. Tiger Woods is the poster boy for on performance. His mastery comes from his focus, mental toughness and practising over and over again the actions he knows will give him success.

PLAN TO TAKE ACTION, AND PLAN THE ACTION THAT YOU WILL TAKE

Some people feel that taking action is reactive and brainless. On the contrary, the most productive action is prepared for and well thought out. Most of us can be placed in one of two categories: Some do only what needs to be done to get by. In other words, they take as little action as possible to maintain the status quo and hope to make the team again next season. Others plan to improve. We plan the action that we are going to take in order to maximize our desired results.

A free lunch is only found in mousetraps.

—John Capozzi, American entrepreneur and author

If we are honest with ourselves, we have all experienced both mindsets. I knew that I was on top of my game when I was as mentally prepared for practice as I was for the game. Most players remember Mike Bossy of the New York Islanders as a great goal scorer, and he was. But most fans did not see the way that Bossy practised for hours and hours, working on the quick release of his wrist shot or half-slapshot after practice.

Bossy was one of the early innovators in his post-practice routine. While the rest of us were trying to pick the corner of the net with our shots in practice, Bossy was purposely shooting for the middle of the net. He recognized that the increased speed of the game did not allow for pretty shots, and he was going to play the odds. Shooting for the middle of the net gave him a higher percentage of shots on net and the opportunity for most of those shots to slip through the middle of the goalie's pads.

Mike Gartner also had an amazing NHL career. I played with Mike in Washington, where we soon became best friends. He turned into an incredible goal scorer whose forte was a fabulous skating stride and speed that backed off opposing defencemen. Yes, Mike possessed a lot of God-given talent (I always thought his advantage came from his bowed legs), but you should have seen the way he applied it! One summer, our families spent time together at the Gartners' cottage in Ontario. I always prided myself on staying in good shape throughout the off-season, and we went on a bike ride as part of our workout. I borrowed a bike and tried to keep up as Mike raced for hours at high speeds along the backcountry roads. Mike Gartner had incredible on-ice speed, but much of it came from the way he kept his skating legs conditioned off the ice. Both Bossy and Gartner didn't just take action—they planned the action that they were going to take.

I once heard the definition of insanity as "doing the same thing we did yesterday, but expecting different results today." Throughout my career, I planned for the action that I was going to take. I noticed in the early '80s that goaltenders were starting to be much more aggressive, moving far out of their nets to take away the shooters' chances to score. Goalies were also starting to take away the bottom of the net with the "butterfly" style. The adjustment that successful scorers in the league were making during this time was to fake a shot and then to move laterally, exposing more open net. This fake became very effective once the goaltenders had committed themselves to moving out of their nets.

It certainly wasn't easy to make this kind of change, though. For years, we would practise shooting the puck at the goalie by skating straight toward him, winding up and letting it rip. To adjust my style, I daily talked myself through practice. Every shot I took in practice I preceded with a fake of some sort. I knew that if I didn't change my action drastically during practice, there was no way the desired action would follow me into the game.

 Ambition is a poor excuse for not having sense enough to be lazy.
—Charlie McCarthy, ventriloquist Edgar Bergen's top-hatted puppet

FINDING YOUR NATURAL GAS

In the oil and gas business, companies try to find energy and sell it. Each of us is in a similar business. We try to find as much energy as possible to sell as performance in the marketplace. Expending energy is the world's national pastime, but we often pay little attention to the first stage—finding the energy to expend. What steps do we personally take to dig our most productive well of energy? Finding the energy necessary to maximize our performance is a skill unto itself.

Two types of energy will dictate how successful our action becomes. The first type is physical. Many talented athletes never give themselves a chance to perform at their highest level, because they don't prioritize developing physical energy reserves. "Burning the candle at both ends" is a popular saying for not knowing when to have fun and when to stop. Planning really helps here. Proper nutrition, rest and exercise energize us for optimum performance. Most professional athletes today hire personal trainers. The reason is simple: human nature. Most of us do what we need to do only when we feel like it. Accountability to someone else helps us do what we need to do even when we don't want to do it.

The key to physical excellence begins with creating a plan with both accountability and flexibility built into it. The bonus along the running, weightlifting or otherwise exercising road is that the more you do, the better you feel. Have you ever noticed the way that your body desires more exercise after you have started to exercise? Our increased action sparks our next level of action. The secret to a successful workout is to simply get started.

The second type of energy that drives our action is desire. It is like a renewable resource—the more we use it, the more it replaces itself. Some people have a bent from birth in this area, but others need to nurture it. This energy comes from a deep hunger to accomplish and succeed. In order to take successful action, we have to want it badly.

 They say a person needs just three things to be truly happy in this world: someone to love, something to do, and something to hope for.
—Thomas Edward Bodett, American author and radio commentator

Playing minor hockey during my formative years provided me with many fond memories. Within my peer group throughout the province of British Columbia, a number of players really stood out for their talent. One player in particular, through his early stages of development, was truly exceptional. He easily moved into junior with success, and he was drafted in the first round to an NHL team.

It is my understanding, however, that soon after being drafted, he quit hockey and went back to school. I heard later that when he was younger, this player's father would take him out of school and force him to skate at the local rink. Maybe it was his dad's dream to play in the NHL and not his own.

In the end, when the puck goes into the corner and the opposing player coming after us is 6 feet 4 inches and 230 pounds, everything boils down to, "How much do we really want it?" Successful action is catalyzed by personal hunger. We have to be the source of our own hunger. Others can't push us into it; we must muster up this hunger within ourselves.

PASSION IS ESSENTIAL

To sustain long-term performance and successful action, there has to be passion. When the desire to accomplish is there, it fuels our passion. Combine action with enthusiasm, and you've got a real potion for success. Professional baseball's Lou Gehrig delivered a long and sustainable performance. He played 2,130 games without missing a single one. During that time, it is said Gehrig had suffered 17 fractures, including breaks in all 10 fingers. When asked why he kept going, his answer was simple and powerful, "Every time I put on the New York Yankee uniform I get excited!" Building sustainable peak performance has a caveat: you have to love what you're doing.

I would rather be ashes than dust! I would rather that my spark should burn out in a brilliant blaze than it should be stifled by dry rot. I would rather be a superb meteor, every atom of me in magnificent glow, than a sleepy and permanent planet. The function of man is to live, not to exist. I shall not waste my days in trying to prolong them. I shall use my time.

—Jack London, American novelist

During our move from the Montreal Canadiens to the Vancouver Canucks, our first order of business was to find a house and property for our young, growing family. We had a dream of building a little hobby farm (as if we needed the extra responsibility) and began looking for an acreage. From the back of our minds to the front of a very poorly fenced two acres, our dreaming evolved into 2 calves, 10 chickens and 2 goats, as well as various dogs and cats.

I am not a good farmer, and we had our share of trying experiences. One of those included one of the calves dying—we still have no idea why. I soon learned that cattle are very gregarious creatures. Boy, was that remaining calf lonely. In very short order, it decided to adopt the two goats as its illegal guardians. The three musketeers became inseparable. Everywhere the goats went so did Gruffy. Everything the goats ate, mostly leaves and tall weeds, Gruffy ate. He actually gave up our open fields of grass for the long, low vines of the old willow tree. The goats taught Gruffy to be a much better escape artist.

Can I say again, "I am not much of a farmer"? Most of the barnyard animals that we have ever entertained have, at one time or another, escaped. So it was only natural that Gruffy would somehow, some way, find a way through the fence. His greatest gift, however, was his timing. I was off on another week-long road trip broadcasting NHL games. My wife, Jenn, had dropped me at the airport and then returned to see Gruffy walking up and down the middle of the road just outside our driveway. Jenn had on a dress and high-heeled shoes and was toting our two-year-old daughter, Emma. Jenn was not impressed.

The beginning of a torrential downpour may have been what broke the camel's back, or at least Gruffy's. Jenn ran, soaking wet, with a bucket of feed, out to the middle of the road to coerce the calf back to our place. But that wasn't the end of it. After capturing him, she picked up the phone and made a very strategic call to the butcher. Rather than enjoying steak à la Gruffy, as we had planned, we had to cry in our Gruffy veal.

What's the moral of the story? Life's actions bring corresponding consequences, and what a consequence for my poor buddy, Gruffy. We need to set our own course within each of our farmyards. When we allow ourselves to be sidetracked into following the goats and eating leaves, we are wasting our time and energy and may be getting ourselves into genuine trouble. Gruffy would have been wise to stick to eating the grass on his own side of the fence, rather than straying outside the boundaries and copying someone who was pursuing a different dream. The consequences of our inaction can be equally devastating, but taking control of our confidence, communication, focus and actions will help us to get where we want to go.

When you change your way of thinking,
  you change your beliefs.
When you change your beliefs,
  you change your expectation.
When you change your expectation,
  you change your attitude.
When you change your attitude,
  you change your behavior, action, and performance.

These first four chapters have dealt with the areas of our lives that we can control:

- Our thought processes
- The things we say
- Where our eyes are focussed
- The actions we take

The importance of these four areas of personal development is spoken of in the ancient, relevant wisdom of the Bible. Hear the book of Proverbs, written many hockey seasons before any of us was born:

> Be careful what you think, because your thoughts run your life.
> Don't use your mouth to tell lies; don't ever say things that are not true.
> Keep your eyes focussed on what is right, and look straight ahead to what is good.
> Be careful what you do, and always do what is right.
>
> —Proverbs 4

If we take charge of the things that we can control, success comes sooner.

In reading the lives of great men, I have found that the first victory they won was over themselves—self-discipline, with all of them, came first.

—Harry S. Truman, former U.S. president

Ryan, in his first two seasons in Montreal, was privileged to play on a
line with Guy Lafleur.

Chapter 5 **Be a Team Player: Choose Team Success**

The important thing to recognize is that it takes a team, and the team ought to get credit for the wins and the losses. Successes have many fathers, failures have none.

—Philip Caldwell, author

HERE'S SOME MORE WISDOM collected from the farmyard. Long-time family friends Dwayne and Sue Lowdermilk thought that acreage would look good with two baby bulls prancing around on the grass. These baby bulls were not yet weaned but had been removed from their mother. When they mooed for milk, I came running with a monster-sized bottle, day or night.

Before I go very much farther, I want to firmly plant this important fact in your minds: I am willing to try almost anything in this wonderful life, but remember this—I am not a very good farmer. It seems that almost everything that can go wrong, does.

One of the two baby bulls gave us a great surprise one evening when we arrived home late after a minor hockey game. As per our normal routine, we counted up the various pieces of livestock we had gathered. "Chickens, goats, yes, there they are; one calf, okay. Now where's the other beast?" From what seemed to be the bottom of a tunnel, or the middle of the earth, we heard this faint, dejected, very distressed "moo."

Everybody was on the hunt now, as dusk was closing in on us. Finally, one of our kids yelled, "Dad! Mom! Charlie's over here, he fell down the culvert!" As far as naming these baby bulls, right from the start we had tried to establish the correct perspective. Their full names were Charlie "Steak" Walter and Gruffy "Roast Beef" Walter. And now Steak was in the culvert. This silly calf was holding on by his hooves and anybody with eyes could see that his upper biceps were tiring. I nearly broke my back pulling this curious calf out. Our little Charlie died later, before we could eat him, and we were all sad. This culvert incident may have had something to do with it.

It was easy to tell I was not a very good farmer by the feeble fences that were supposed to keep the animals separate from the rest of us. My fences were temporary, and the animals figured this out within a short period of time. During this time, our family dog was Aslan, a golden retriever. I still have warm memories of that dog. Aslan lived with us during the Montreal Canadien days, and he wagged his tail every time I came home from games where the 18,000 fans at the Forum had just screamed at me to "go home, and then keep driving!" Through the pressure days of playing in Montreal, whether I hit or missed empty nets, my buddy Aslan (along with my wife) was happy to see me.

What did Aslan do by nature? He retrieved! Now this wouldn't have been a problem unless we lived next to a golf course. We did. Every morning, a group of elderly men played an early round of golf and then ate breakfast together at the little clubhouse. Before they went in, each took off his golf shoes. I think you see where this is heading. Every morning, Aslan would show up on our front porch with one golf shoe—and one time, a pair of pants! These men thought one of their group was playing games with the rest of them. Every afternoon, I would sneak the golf shoe back to the clubhouse.

Our 10 chickens were focussed on one important mission and they tried to fulfill it each morning. All 10 were in "escape and lay" mode. The first part of their mission was to get through or over Farmer Ryan's fence and then, as quickly as possible, move strategically to the first tee of the golf course, where they would happily lay their eggs among the range balls. The embarrassing part of their mission, for us, was that they would not come home. Every day, we had to go and shoo them home, uttering apologies to golfers and course keepers alike. It keeps you humble.

Here are the significant thoughts that come out of the Funny Farm. Each player in a family, a business or on a professional sports team has an individual personality and a specific set of skills. For some reason, in the context of wanting to be a team player, we pick out a teammate and then try to do what he or she does.

Being a team player does not mean that you change what you bring to the table. If you're a retriever, bring the shoes to the porch! If you're a chicken, lay eggs at the golf course. And if you are like Gruffy the wayward bull, do your best just to stay out of trouble.

Working hard for a win, some people make the mistake of trying to be what they are not. In the game of hockey, we have a saying: "If you're a dancer, dance." If you're a goal scorer, score. If you're a set-up man, move the puck. If you're a tough player, play tough. The whole concept of being a team player doesn't come easily to people. Nevertheless, good teams start out with individuals and end up with players committed to achieving together what they could never have accomplished on their own.

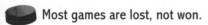 **Most games are lost, not won.**

—Casey Stengal, American baseball manager

One of the greatest personal challenges of my hockey career came, as I mentioned before, when I broke my ankle with four games to go in the 1985–86 season. This injury would keep me from playing during the Stanley Cup playoffs.

The first week was painful but also exhilarating, as Jenn and I welcomed our second child, Christiana, into the world. As time went on, the pain in my ankle moved to my heart. Our team was doing the unexpected: winning. I was proud and excited as my buddies beat the Hartford Whalers in seven games. It took Claude Lemieux's goal in sudden-death overtime to accomplish this second-round victory, and it seemed to fuel the momentum needed for the team to be successful in the post-season.

I tried to enjoy watching the games until, during the last part of the series, I was finally given the okay to begin working out with my legs again. Up to that point, I had invented my own system to keep up my conditioning. I flipped over an exercise bike in the dressing room and pedalled with my arms. It pumped my arms up so much that it started a new trend on our team! Meanwhile, our second-round victory over Hartford propelled our team to and then past the New York Rangers. All of a sudden, the 1986 version of the Montreal Canadiens was preparing to face off against the Calgary Flames for the Stanley Cup.

Every team bone in my body was challenged. The 1985–86 regular season had seen me play a prominent role on our side. Now, in the post-season, my team was having incredible success without me. I wanted to be contributing to the triumphs of our team, and all I could do was watch from the sidelines. I wanted to share in the exhilaration of winning each round in the playoffs with the boys, and all I could do was shake the guys' hands after games and offer my congratulations.

What I did discover during this difficult time was a different perspective on being a team player. For the first time in my professional life, I was forced to examine my attitudes and motives in this area. Was I really happy for the players on our team when they had success? Could I contribute to the positive team atmosphere, even while playing a much-reduced role? The view that I was getting for the first time was from the periphery, rather than the inside, and it was an uncomfortable place.

This was a period of great personal development for me. I learned some things about myself and about really being a team player. I mustered all the mental toughness that I had developed over the years to keep my attitude on-stream and in-line. Instead of complaining outwardly of my woes, I chose to encourage my buddies during every conversation. I emphasized the positive to them, even though my heart was longing to be in their position. I had to find a way to redirect these feelings of jealousy toward the very guys I was closest to.

The workouts in the back room got longer and more intense. This was my only release for the feelings that I knew I shouldn't have. The guys must have thought I had gone bonkers. I got to the point where I wouldn't watch the games in the stands or the press box. As my teammates were working on the ice, I would work off the ice. The TV in the workout room kept me current, and the workout equipment kept my heart, mind and body distracted from those feelings of jealousy.

The lessons I learned about being a team player while pedalling with my arms were very profitable. I learned to be much more inclusive toward players on my team who play a lesser or more peripheral role. I learned the value of building up people of lesser status on my team. Through this time, I learned to appreciate the team dynamic more and, from the edge, observed what worked and what didn't. I also experienced a foreshadowing of retirement from this game that I had always played. I know many professional athletes who have struggled in their post-career adjustment because, for the first time in their lives, they have had to play a different team role. It's easy to be a team player when you are the star or the president of the company. Your self-esteem is stroked because of your personal success, so talking the good "team talk" is easy. It's different when you are in the back seat.

As my teammates continued to win, I also learned from them. Some of my buddies had no time or energy for my personal situation. I was like a piece of the furniture in the back workout room to say good morning to before walking to the 25 waiting reporters in the dressing room. But most of my teammates showed great empathy for my situation and asked often how I was doing, and they included me as our team walked down this winning road.

> **Our true character is illuminated by the way we treat the janitor of the company, not the president or CEO.**

There is an interesting ending to this story. My attempt to have a good team attitude while working my frustrations out on the bike paid off. By keeping myself in good shape mentally and physically, I had put myself in a prepared position. Our orthopaedic surgeon, Eric Lenzner, whispered to me during one visit that if the pain wasn't too bad, he might give me the okay to play. Days before the final playoff series with Calgary, I began to skate for the first time in two months, and our head coach, Jean Perron, invited me to participate in the five games that it took for us to win the Cup.

Even superstars in the game of hockey recognize the importance of every player. When Markus Naslund was named captain of the Vancouver Canucks, members of the media asked him if it was going to be hard to fill the shoes of Mark Messier, the previous team captain. Naslund answered, "Of course! Mark may be the most respected player and captain in recent hockey history."

Naslund was then asked if there was anything Messier did as captain that he would try to emulate. Naslund replied, "Yes, in the way he treated the players. Mark Messier recognized the need for each player on a successful team and had as much time for the fourth-line players as the first-line guys."

I still have much more to learn about being a complete team player. I do know these things:

- Everyone plays on a team, whether it is in sports, business, friendships or family.
- Developing a "team player" attitude is just as important as developing physical skills.
- Success is hollow unless you have teammates to share it with.

FOUR WAYS TO ENHANCE OUR TEAM APPROACH

1 Polish our people skills.

The way we learn to interact with others often defines not only our success, but also our enjoyment of life.

Theodore Roosevelt: The most important single ingredient in the formula of success is knowing how to get along with people.

John D. Rockefeller: I will pay more for the ability to deal with people than any other ability under the sun.

J.P. Getty: It doesn't make a difference how much knowledge or experience an executive possesses; if he is unable to achieve results through people, he is worthless as an executive.

J.A. Holmes: It is wise to remember that the entire population of the universe, with one trifling exception, is composed of others.

These successful men have articulated that our individual success often depends on how we view and interact with our teammates. The Stanford Research Institute found that the money you make in any endeavour is determined only 12.5 percent by knowledge and 87.5 percent by your ability to deal with people.

Interacting with others is not easy for some, and I am not asking anyone to step outside his or her individual personality. Nevertheless, learn to enjoy people, especially your teammates. Make time to talk. Be interested in their lives. The speaker, author and salesman Zig Ziglar built an empire on these words: "You can have everything you want in life, if you help enough people get what they want!" He goes on to say that you must show interest in others as a first step.

We are, if nothing else, a hockey family. My parents deserve much of the credit for my NHL career, because they endured the early morning practices and the long trips to watch our games, with little time left for themselves. I played junior hockey, and my brother George followed along behind me. After junior, I was very fortunate to be drafted and move right into a career in hockey at the professional level. George also went to a pro camp with the Washington Capitals. He decided that if the Caps were to send him down to the International Hockey League, their lowest farm team, he would pack in hockey and start a new career path. The team wanted him to go to "the I." George, true to his word, packed up his hockey equipment, bought a commercial fishing boat and started down a new path.

People might say that George's junior hockey career was a waste of time and energy. He spent his teenage years getting traded throughout the Western Hockey League, when he could have been pursuing a higher education. But during the time that George spent riding on buses from city to town across western Canada, he learned a huge life skill: how to get along with people. George has built an awesome business through his street smarts and acumen but most of all by his friendly, gregarious approach to his customers and clients. Crammed into the back of those old buses, travelling day and night, players are forced to learn how to get along with, and maybe even enjoy, each other. We have all benefited from being on teams where nobody's perfect and personalities clash. Team players learn how to work it out.

Note how good you feel after you have encouraged someone else. No other argument is necessary to suggest that you never miss the opportunity to give encouragement.

—George Burton Adams, English historian and author

Former New Jersey Devils coach Larry Robinson replaced head coach Robbie Ftorek near the end of the 1999–2000 NHL season. His team went on to win the Stanley Cup in 2000. Having played with Robinson in Montreal, I was not surprised to hear that his genuine ability to laugh and enjoy the players he was coaching may have put them over the top. In fact, during the Eastern Conference series against the Philadelphia Flyers, the Devils were down three games to none when "the speech" took place.

Some coaches raise the roof with their shouting, trying to shock their players into better play. Larry Robinson did the opposite. He pleaded with his players, instilling the belief that they could beat the Flyers even though they were on the brink of elimination. After Robinson was finished talking to the team, they were not beaten down. They were motivated and ready to get back on the ice. The rest is history, as the Devils devastated the Flyers over the next four games and won the Stanley Cup from the defending champion Dallas Stars.

Napoleon Bonaparte said, "Men are moved by two levers only: fear and self-interest." At times, a good wake-up call is what some of us need in life. Negative motivation, however, should be on the menu only once in a while. People who are good with other people learn to interact, get to know their interests and build up a foundation of trust. There are two types of construction crews: those who build and those who destroy. People are the world's most important asset. We need to find ways to build them up.

2 Place a high value on people.

Baseball great Bob Ueker said the highlight of his career came one clear evening when he saw a man reach for a fly ball and actually fall out of the upper deck, land and miraculously get up and walk away. What amazed Ueker was that the crowd booed the man because he had bobbled the ball.

Performance in professional sports and life is important, but the performance must be separated from the person. During my fourth season in the NHL, I had a terrific year, scoring 38 goals. I was reaching a certain status, and some people wanted to hang out with me just in case my status continued to spiral upward. During my 15th season, I scored only three goals. The prestige had fallen away, and most friends and acquaintances that I had by this time were genuine. In the life of a team it becomes really important for players to know that even when their performance dries up for a while, their teammates will not distance themselves. Differentiating between people and their performance is one of the hardest things that we will ever do, but it is a sure indicator of the value we place on people.

You're not a bad person just because you shoot a bad score. You just need to keep plugging and realize that there will be better days ... I know that there is more to life than golf, I can put it in perspective.

—Dawn Coe-Jones, Canadian golfer

In a conversation I enjoyed with then Los Angeles Kings coach Andy Murray, we talked about the Kings' early success during that season, and then I inquired about a young rookie, Steven Reinprecht. Murray's eyes lit up and he went into great detail not only about Reinprecht's on-ice ability but also his character. Murray told me the following story to highlight his point: At the end of practice, the Kings often had a shootout to add some fun to their long season. Each skater would get a breakaway shot from the red line in on one of the goalies. This is where the Kings added a wrinkle: Murray divided the two sides of the rink into a "he will score" side and a "he will not score" side. Before each player took his shot, the rest of the skaters had to choose a side, showing confidence or not in the particular player's scoring ability. To add to the choice, if players moved to the "he will score" side of the ice and the player didn't score, those players who believed that he would had to skate laps around the ice as the consequence. Here's where Reinprecht came in. As a rookie wanting to show respect for the older players on the team, he picked the "he will score" side every time. More often than not Reinprecht had to skate laps because of his choice. Early in the season the players and coaching staff did not catch on to Reinprecht's strategy, but when they did, they were all very impressed with this young man's character and commitment to the team.

Close friends love you for who you are, not what they want you to be.

—Ted Rall, American editorial cartoonist

3. Develop an atmosphere of sacrifice.

Abraham Lincoln was walking with two of his boys one day. They were both whining and crying. A friend came up to Lincoln and asked, "What's the matter with the boys?" Lincoln replied, "The same thing that's wrong with the whole world: I've got three walnuts, and they both want two."

Most of us want the walnuts, and we want them now. Personally sacrificing the walnut for a teammate is hard in our "I'm the greatest" culture, but it is necessary in building a team.

A young girl named Lisa had a rare and serious disease, and the doctors felt that her only chance for survival would come from a blood transfusion from her five-year-old brother, who had beaten the disease earlier and whose blood now carried the antibodies. The doctors asked the boy if he would be willing to give his blood to his sister.

He hesitated for only a moment before taking a deep breath and saying, "Yes, I'll do it if it will save Lisa." As the transfusion progressed, he looked at his sister and smiled, as everyone could see the colour come back into her cheeks. Then he looked at the doctor and asked with a trembling voice, "Will I start to die right away?" He had misunderstood the doctors and thought he must give all of his blood so that his sister could live. Not many of us in sports or in life are asked to sacrifice to the point of death, but little sacrifices for our teammates can have a huge impact on the chemistry of our team.

At the beginning of my second NHL season with the Washington Capitals, our team was experimenting with a number of different players to see if they could help the Caps improve. During the exhibition schedule, I was put on a line with a young player who had a number of years of experience in the minors but had never been able to crack the NHL. During the games that we played together he always talked about the goals he had scored in the past, intimating that if the other winger and I did the dirty work in the corners and got him the puck, he would do the scoring. The sad thing was that this player was very talented and should have played many seasons in the NHL, but he only played for a couple of months and petered out. I found it interesting that this player and others before and after him had sufficient talent to impress the general manager and even the coach for a little while, but his attitude surfaced quickly in the trenches with his teammates. You can't fool the people that you eat and sleep and compete with every day for eight or nine months of the year. I learned from this unfortunate athlete that if you sacrifice for your teammate, eventually he will sacrifice for you. If you take the easy road on the sweat of his back, however, you will have a difficult time achieving your goals.

The story of the Good Samaritan is a powerful illustration of sacrificial action. A young man was walking the road from Jerusalem to Jericho when thieves jumped him, took his possessions, beat him badly and left him for dead. A little while later, a Jewish priest using the same road saw the victim lying injured and walked on by. Later in the day, a Levite did the same thing. Finally, a Samaritan happened upon the young man. He had compassion on him, placed him on his donkey, took him to an inn and paid the bill, telling the owner that he would return to pay whatever expenses the victim incurred in his recovery. While those who should have helped the injured man walked by, the Good Samaritan used his time and resources to help someone else. On our teams, we need to be contributors, not consumers, even when it means personal sacrifice.

The story of the Good Samaritan can be summarized this way: The thief, in essence, says, "What's yours is mine, and I'll take it." The priest and Levite, by their actions, say, "What's mine is mine, and I'll keep it." The Good Samaritan demonstrates an attitude of, "What's mine is yours, and I'll give it."

4 Deflect the glory—build the team.

Professional sports management consistently admonishes players to "be responsible for your performance and your team." Coaches are always talking to their players about bearing the responsibility. Obviously, when players take ownership of their team, when they really buy in to the "I'm responsible for the type of team that we will have" mantra, their play demonstrates an increased level of commitment and consistency.

Paul "Bear" Bryant, the legendary college football coach, wisely added to this concept. Bear referred to himself as an old plowboy. "But," he said, "I know how to build a team."

He said, plain and simple:

"If anything goes bad, I did it.
If anything goes semi-good, we did it.
If anything goes really good, you did it."

You can accomplish a lot in this world if you don't care who gets the credit. Take the responsibility, and share the glory. Coach Bear Bryant really nailed this "personal responsibility" thing on the head. And Bear didn't stop there. To personal responsibility he added what I call deflecting the glory. In individual sports, where the athlete is responsible for his own performance, individuals get all the credit when things go well. In team situations, we can become confused between personal performance and team success. Bear Bryant was correct, though. If we are committed to building a successful team, we need to model deflection, and it typically starts from the top of the organization and filters down.

John Wooden was one of the early coaches to introduce this deflection theme. He told his basketball players that every time they drained a basket, they should turn and point at the player who gave them the assist. In other words, acknowledge that others worked hard to get you the ball, and share the credit for the basket.

My own professional sport experience has driven this principle home. Many athletes do a very good job with their team talk, and it shows up on the sports pages of the local newspapers. When the media ask a player to describe one of his or her incredible feats, a quick reminder to self to be inclusive (of teammates and their contributions) and not exclusive (talk only about all the great things I did) will build the team.

I have found that this principle of deflection works well in other areas. I have to remind myself to be inclusive. When talking about our children and their accomplishments (as we all do), we have a tendency to refer to them in this way: "My son, Ben, did this and this and this." I am very conscious of this now and work on always referring to him as, "Our son, Ben." This is such a simple example, but I find that when we are talking about any part of our lives (other than those areas of personal responsibility) it pays real dividends to stay in the plural:

"We did this."
"Our family built that."
"My wife and I helped here."

When we deflect to teammates what we could have taken as personal glory, we build our team.

Ryan checking a great leader, Steve Yzerman of the Detroit Red Wings.

Chapter 6 **Be a Team Leader: Choose to Lead**

Leaders are the custodians of a nation's ideals, of the beliefs it cherishes, of its permanent hopes, of the faith which makes a nation out of a mere aggregation of individuals!

—Walter Lippmann, American journalist and author

EVERY PERSON GETS A SHOT at being a leader. Mothers, fathers, friends, siblings, players, coaches, presidents and CEOs share this experience. Leaders are not born, they're built. The trick is to learn how to lead well and to discover a leadership style that's effective for you.

A study by Thor Thorlindsson, at the University of Iceland, found that 40 percent of the variation in the herring catch (among his country's 200-plus fishing fleets) was due entirely to the ability of the captain. Another study of large corporations over a four-year period, by three scholars at the Wharton School of business at the University of Pennsylvania, concluded that between 15 and 25 percent of the variation in profitability was determined by the character of the companies' chief executives. As Professor Robert J. House of Wharton concluded, "We're learning again what the military has known for years; leadership is important."

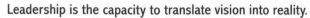 **Leadership is the capacity to translate vision into reality.**
> —Warren G. Bennis, American management professor

Michael E. Heisley Sr. is a very wealthy man; the Vancouver (now Memphis) Grizzlies of the National Basketball Association became one of his companies. Heisley grew up in Alexandria, Virginia, in a relatively poor family. He and his wife had their five children in the first seven years of marriage. During their third year of marriage, Heisley was making $5,000 a year as a computer salesman. The Heisleys moved to Chicago in 1979, took the $150,000 capital that they received from selling their house and invested it in a distressed manufacturing company in Mendota, Illinois. Says Heisley, "I straightened that company out, then took the profit and used it to borrow money to buy another company that was in trouble." Heisley repeated the process over the years, until he made a fine art out of swooping down like some rescue angel, buying failing businesses, then transforming and reviving them through an ingenious system of study, reorganization and improved methods of management and production.

Even more impressive than the way he saved businesses was the way he saved people's jobs. Part of his formula is to minimize laying people off, unless absolutely necessary. Heisley says, "The way you make a company better is by increasing the productivity of the workers. If you demoralize the employees, it is very difficult to get them to produce more products."

 It's only when we develop others that we permanently succeed.
> —Harvey Firestone, American industrialist

Former U.S. president Dwight Eisenhower defined leadership as "the art of getting someone else to do something that you want done, because he wants to do it." The last part of that sentence may be the most important. The challenge is to move people into a space where they want to do it. You may have heard the following story before.

AT THE GYM

One Christmas, my wife purchased me a week of private lessons at the local health club. Though still in great shape from when I was on the varsity chess team in high school, I decided it was a good idea to go ahead and try it. I called and made reservations with someone named Tanya, who said she was a 26 year-old aerobics instructor and athletic-clothing model. My wife seemed pleased with how enthusiastic I was to get started.

DAY 1
They suggested I keep an exercise diary to chart my progress this week. Started this morning at 6:00 a.m. Tough to get up, but worth it when I arrived at the health club and Tanya was waiting for me. She's something of a goddess, with blond hair and a dazzling white smile. She showed me the machines and took my pulse after five minutes on the treadmill. She seemed alarmed that it was so high, but I think just standing next to her added about 10 points. Enjoyed watching the aerobics class. Tanya was very encouraging as I did my sit-ups, though my stomach was already aching a little from holding it in the whole time I was talking to her. This is going to be great.

DAY 2
Took a whole pot of coffee to get me out the door, but I made it. Tanya had me lie on my back and push this heavy iron bar up into the air. Then she put weights on it, for heaven's sake! Legs were a

little wobbly on the treadmill, but I made it the full mile. Her smile made it all worth it. Muscles feel great.

DAY 3

The only way I can brush my teeth is by lying the toothbrush on the counter and moving my mouth back and forth over it. Driving was okay, as long as I didn't try to steer. Tanya was a little impatient with me and said my screaming was bothering the other club members. The treadmill hurt, so I did the Stair Monster. Why would anyone invent a machine to simulate an activity rendered obsolete by the invention of elevators? Tanya told me regular exercise would make me live longer. I can't imagine anything worse.

DAY 4

Tanya was waiting for me with her vampire teeth in full snarl. I can't help it if I was half an hour late—it took me that long just to tie my shoes. She wanted me to lift dumbbells. Not a chance, Tanya. The word "dumb" must be there for a reason. I hid in the men's room until she sent Lars looking for me. As a punishment, she made me try the rowing machine. It sank.

DAY 5

I hate Tanya more than any human being has ever hated any other human being in the history of the world. She thought it would be a good idea to work on my triceps. Well, I have news for you, Tanya! I don't have any triceps. And if you don't want dents in the floor, don't hand me any barbells. I refuse to accept responsibility for the damage. You went to sadist school. You are to blame. The treadmill flung me back into a science teacher, which hurt like crazy. Why couldn't it have been someone softer, like a music teacher, or social studies?

DAY 6

Got Tanya's message on my answering machine, wondering where I am. I lacked the strength to use the TV remote so I watched 11 straight hours of the weather channel.

DAY 7

Well, that's the week. I'm glad that's over. Maybe next time my wife will give me something a little more fun, like free teeth drilling at the dentist.

This fun story helps highlight two important points. Tanya was unsuccessful as a leader in this relationship because she was unable (despite all of her outward qualities) to motivate her client to meet his goals. Eisenhower's definition is significant: get someone to do something that you want done "because he wants to do it." Leaders can use the lever of fear to motivate occasionally, but over the long run leaders must capture their followers' interest. The second point is simple and equally significant: not all players belong on the leader's team. Unmotivated players will work their way off a leader's team at times because, simply, that's their choice.

I once flew from Vancouver to southern California with a gentleman who pinpointed precisely what went wrong between Tanya and her pupil. We talked about people and motivation. He said his old rowing coach, Neil Casey, had a good saying: "I can teach anyone how to row, but if they don't want to pull, I can't help them."

 A ship in port is safe, but that's not what ships are built for.
—Grace Hopper, American computer scientist and naval officer

 No man was ever endowed with a right without being at the same time saddled with a responsibility.
—Gerald W. Johnson, author

Author and pastor John Maxwell articulates one of the clearest definitions of leadership that I have come across. He simply says, "Leadership is influence!" One of the reasons I like this definition is that I believe it to be powerfully true. The other reason for my excitement over this insightful statement is that its premise is that we are all leaders. Whether we accept the responsibility for this or not, if we have influence over another person we are in a leadership position and need to develop our leadership skills.

Here are four defining statements from the world of sports that fit into the world of everything:

1 Great leaders motivate.

There is no definitive rulebook on motivation. Leaders need to be flexible and able to adjust as situations arise. Issues of change never come easily at the National Hockey League level, nor should they. This great game that I am thankful to have had the opportunity to play through the '70s, '80s and into the '90s is an awesome sporting spectacle. During those years and through the twenty-first century, "sustainable change" continues to dominate the NHL landscape.

During the late '70s, when I broke into the NHL as a centre/winger, the wingers were admonished constantly to limit their scope of movement to up and down their side of the ice. The influence of European hockey and the Edmonton Oilers' style of play in the early '80s changed these limitations on wingers forever, for everyone's benefit and playing pleasure. Similarly, players in today's game grew up with a unique background and therefore have different trigger points when it comes to what will motivate them. As new generations with new backgrounds and new baggage come into the workforce, leaders will have to be flexible in their motivational approach.

Feelings of worth can flourish only in an atmosphere where individual differences are appreciated, mistakes are tolerated, communication is open, and rules are flexible—the kind of atmosphere that is found in a nurturing family.

—Virginia Satir, American family therapist

Winston Churchill said, "I would rather be right than consistent." Churchill often changed his mind or came to a different perspective about old opinions, based on what he called "new facts." As new information is disseminated, leaders understand the need to filter this information and quickly decide what change in their course of action, if any, should be taken.

Thomas Jefferson has a useful phrase that I have leaned on when trying to filter new information: "In matters of style, swim with the current; in matters of principle, stand like a rock!"

Leaders need to develop the ability to differentiate between principle and style. My wife and I always wanted to build a log home, and we realized this dream. Those of you who have been through the process know that plenty of timely decisions must be made. I came to rely on Jefferson's simple thinking when making these decisions. Most things we pondered were issues of style, which I often left to Jenn, since I generally held no strong preference. If she wanted the boys' room to be painted a certain shade of blue, go for it! However, we worked together on issues of principle, like the bottom line.

Leaders need to defer to the players' preferences in style issues that won't affect the outcome of the game. Wise parents have learned that the length, colour or absence of their teenagers' hair is merely a style issue and save their objections for the bigger issues that really matter.

2 Great leaders model.

Players and coaches who motivated me first *were*, before they *said* or *did*. During my final season as a player in the NHL, I dressed for only 25 of the 82 games that our team played. When a player does not participate in the game he has two options: he can either work out in the dressing room or watch the game from the press box. Well into the season, we were at Madison Square Garden to play the Rangers, and I wasn't dressing for this one. In Madison Square, the press box is way up high, but unlike many other buildings, in this one the fans sit right in front of the media. The game was going really well for our team and, as you can imagine, the Ranger fans were getting impatient. The referee, Kerry Fraser, had made a number of calls against the Ranger players, and this helped to move the New York fans from impatient to obnoxious.

Directly in front of my seat in the press box, I spotted three buddies in their early 30s, and I could see that one of them had brought along his 9- or 10-year-old son. As referee Fraser continued with his very warranted calls against the Rangers, the crowd in unison rose to its feet and, as only they can do, began to chant, "Fraser sucks! Fraser sucks!" I was watching these three buddies really getting into this chant, and the son was taking it all in. Eventually, in the spirit of collective referee bashing, this young lad rose to his feet and, next to his dad, in as loud a voice as he could muster, joined in, "Fraser sucks! Fraser sucks!"

I will never forget what happened next. The dad, now recognizing his son's participation, turned to him and harshly said, "No, not you! Sit down!" Then he turned back with his buddies and continued to scream, "Fraser sucks!" The boy slunk back into his seat and bowed his head. I could just imagine what was going on in his heart.

I don't mean to jump specifically on this dad. I have made poor decisions with our children many times (just ask them). But the most powerful way to deliver a message is to model it. People may doubt what you say, but not what you do!

When modelling, a leader needs to be a thermostat, not a thermometer. Like a thermometer, most people are good at telling others the temperature in the room. Walking into any environment, it's easy to observe and complain about the heat. Effective leaders are thermostats: they change the temperature, instead of complaining about it. They find a solution and implement it. When we model being part of the solution, those around us learn how to be part of it too. These people then become our next generation of leaders.

3 Great leaders place trust.

My mother and father were really good at a lot of things, but they excelled in the area of placing trust. I was the type of kid who wanted to drive a car the minute I turned 16 years old. I saved most of my paper-route money, and it was just barely enough to buy an old panel truck with a starter on the floor. I really enjoyed the truck, and my folks were smart to let me buy it. The old beast was practically indestructible, which was perfect for a 16-year-old male. After my birthday in April, I passed my driving test, and with a watch-out-world attitude I took to the streets. I won't bore you with the accounts of the near accidents that occurred; I just want you to know that I remember my mom and dad allowing me to share the driving on our family vacation that summer.

Our family of six, plus the dog, always camped north of Vancouver, high in the mountains of the Cariboo, and the only way to get there was via the Fraser Canyon. The road follows the mighty Fraser River and dips and dives ferociously. To put it bluntly, a young driver could easily make a fatal mistake. My folks demonstrated their trust in me by allowing me to share in the driving. Placing trust builds trust.

My father gave me a favourite plaque of his when I was going through a difficult time in business. It quotes Ralph Waldo Emersion: "The glory of friendship is not the outstretched hand, nor the kindly smile nor the joy of companionship; it is the spiritual inspiration that comes to one when he discovers that someone else believes in him, and is willing to trust him."

I define trust as "the people glue" or "the team epoxy." General George Patton's soldiers undoubtedly felt his trust in them. "I never tell people how to do something," he said. "I tell them what I need done, and then I look forward to their ingenuity."

My first NHL training camp was a tough one, because I missed it. Just weeks before the start of camp I was at home in Vancouver, and I was passing a lacrosse ball with my brother in the backyard when I twisted and pulled the cartilage in my left knee. Knee operations back in those days were not orthoscopic in nature. The doctor removed the whole cartilage and told me not to move much. Of course, the longer we sit still, the longer the rehabilitation process.

By the time I was ready, the Washington Capitals were playing the regular season, and my first game was in the old Chicago Stadium. Near the end of the game, tied 2–2 with under a minute remaining, the faceoff was in our end, to the left of our goalie. I thought Dan Belisle, my first NHL coach, was making a mistake when he kept calling my name. I turned around and he said, "Go get the faceoff, kid." With time running out, Dan was counting on me in my first NHL game. It gets worse. After entering the faceoff circle, I looked up, and whom did I see? Stan Mikita, the Black Hawks' legendary centreman. Fortunately for me, I tied up Stan's stick, we tied the faceoff, and our team tied the game. My coach placed trust in me.

As I was writing this chapter, I happened to bump into Dan Belisle in Philadelphia, where he was scouting for the Detroit Red Wings and I was broadcasting the game for TV. I asked him if he remembered the situation. Not only did he remember, but he also added a perspective that I had not thought of. Belisle felt that I had been the strongest on faceoffs that night, so to put me on the ice was natural, but in getting me on the ice, he pulled the Guy Charron line off. Charron was a veteran player and Belisle said, all those years later, "If I had a chance to do that line change over again, I would have put you at centre, Ryan, and left Guy on as a left-winger. I put you in a position to build your confidence, but I lost Guy's confidence when I took him off the ice in such a critical situation." This is fascinating insight from an NHL coach on how to build and maintain the confidence of players.

 The new leader is a facilitator, not an order giver.
—John Naisbitt, American futurist and author

4 Great leaders cheerlead.

In *Money* magazine a number of years ago, Ken Blanchard described the "gung-ho" revolution. "Gung-ho" as Blanchard applied it means "work together." He explains that even though everybody bangs the people-are-important drum, all too often we treat those same people with less care and respect than we do paper and pens. People are not as productive as they could be because of what Blanchard calls the "seagull management" style, which he says is the most utilized style in America today.

In seagull management, "managers are not around very much. But when they hear something is wrong, they fly in, make a lot of noise, dump on everyone and they fly out." Blanchard goes on to say, "The mathematics of this system doesn't work. The employee figures out very fast that the less work you do, the less chance of you being wrong or making a mistake, and therefore there is less chance that you will get 'zinged' by your boss." The spark that flames the gung-ho revolution, Blanchard says, is simple: "Cheer one another on!" To create excited, enthusiastic employees, "Catch them doing something right, and then cheer them on."

Whether we are building a Stanley Cup contending team, a solid dot-com business or the most important team of all—our families—Ken Blanchard's words are pure gold. Catch people doing something right, and cheer them on! This doesn't always come naturally. I have found that even with my wife, the person closest to me, I need to affirm many of the good things accomplished in the day, instead of noticing if the dishes didn't get washed. This works both ways in our relationship.

 Flatter me, and I may not believe you. Criticize me, and I may not like you. Ignore me, and I may not forgive you. Encourage me, and I will not forget you.
—William Arthur Ward, American author and educator

One practical way that a friend of mine, Roger Neilson, cheered was through sending cards. Neilson coached at the NHL level for two generations of players and everyone in hockey knew him. During his fatal battle with cancer, when I should have been sending him encouraging messages, he was writing to me. In today's world of e-everything, the card mailed through the regular post remains powerful.

Outstanding leaders go out of their way to boost the self-esteem of their personnel. If people believe in themselves, it's amazing what they can accomplish.
—Sam Walton, American retailing executive

Another friend, Don Liesemer, who is president of Hockey Ministries International, has amazing timing with his telephone calls. Just when I need him, he's there, cheering me on. Cheerleaders are supportive to a fault and incredibly enthusiastic. We all need people like that in our lives. We all need to be people like that in the lives of others.

A TRUE NORTH

Our ships are tossed
Across the night,
Our compass cracked,
For wrong or right.
True North is there,
Or over here?
Confusion rules
Our sea is fear.
Then suddenly, a beacon bright
Is shining through
This stormy night.
It's pure and straight
To his true course.
The coach is seen.
He is True North.

—Steve Jamison

Be true north—motivate, model, trust, encourage. As you influence in a positive way, you are serving those around you, rather than yourself.

Service to others is the rent you pay for your room here on earth.

—Muhammad Ali, American boxer

Ryan celebrates a goal during Washington's first-ever victory
over Montreal.

Chapter 7 **Be a Winner: The Choice is Yours**

The miracle, or the power, that elevates the few is to be found in their industry, application and perseverance, under the prompting of a brave, determined spirit.

—Mark Twain, American writer and humorist

I AM CONVINCED that a huge advantage to playing sports is experiencing first-hand the lessons it has to teach about life. Walter Payton of the Chicago Bears ran over 11 miles with the ball during his 13-year pro football career, while getting knocked down every couple of feet. This is a great visual presentation of the principle of perseverance.

From the age of 19 until I was 34 years old, I played 1,003 NHL games. Winning and losing, and then preparing to win again, develops a mindset that I believe is key not only to succeeding in life but also to enjoying life. Perhaps the critical principle that I packed in my briefcase when I exchanged my NHL jersey for a business suit is that there will be seasons of winning, seasons of losing and seasons of injury; but through all of these times, players must develop the courage to view a failure or a loss as a "regrouping opportunity" that launches them forward toward their goal.

The greater part of happiness or misery depends on our dispositions, not our circumstances.

—Martha Washington, former U.S. first lady

At every level of achievement stands a trophy. Some people reach a certain level and then quit, because to keep going demands too much commitment. Others take past failures personally and are unable to move forward. Most people don't realize that the ebb and flow of winning and losing teaches us to persevere and prods us slowly onward, toward our goals.

Winning in life is a process to be enjoyed. When I look back on winning a Stanley Cup, the final game is a great memory, but not the only one. It takes 82 regular-season games of preparation, coupled with winning the best of seven games four times, to reach that pinnacle. I can't just point to the pinnacle and say, "That did it for us." No, it was the winning and losing and the challenge of readjusting the strategy that stands out just as strongly in my memory as holding the Stanley Cup.

 If you don't make mistakes, you aren't really trying.

—Coleman Hawkins, American jazz saxophonist

 Don't be afraid to go out on a limb. That's where the fruit is.

—H. Jackson Brown Jr., American marketer and author

This attitude of perseverance is powerfully evident in those people who are fighting debilitating illnesses. This power of stick-to-itiveness is the bulldog-type that I so admire in Winston Churchill and others who soldiered on as war played out on the world scene. This is the life skill of "failing forward": using failures to propel us onward instead of giving up. Perhaps nothing could encourage us more to fail forward than reviewing the events of Abraham Lincoln's life:

- Difficult childhood
- Less than one year of formal schooling
- Failed in business in 1831
- Defeated in run for Illinois legislature, '32
- Failed in business, '33
- Elected to Illinois legislature, '34
- Fiancée died, '35
- Re-elected to Illinois legislature, '36
- Re-elected to Illinois legislature but defeated in bid to be
- Speaker, '38
- Re-elected to Illinois legislature but defeated in bid to be
- Elector, '40
- Married, '42; marriage troubled at times
- Lost three of his four sons before they were 19
- Defeated in bid for U.S. Congress, '43
- Elected to U.S. House of Representatives, '46
- Defeated in bid for Senate, '55
- Defeated in bid for vice-president, '56
- Defeated in bid for Senate, '58
- Elected president, '60

Success is not final, failure is not fatal; it is the courage to continue that counts.
—Winston Churchill, former British prime minister, statesman and author

As our teams compete, life dictates that on the horizon are peaks and valleys that we must traverse. Teams, companies and families need players with the courage to persevere. For me, the peaks of success have usually come on the heels of what I thought at the time was near disaster: ruining my knees, breaking my ankle, and the list goes on. This is why it is important to keep the "big picture" in mind, never allowing a temporary failure to stand in the way of forward momentum.

The measure of a man is the way he bears up under misfortune.

—Plutarch, Greek biographer and moralist

Patience and perseverance have a magical effect before which difficulties disappear and obstacles vanish.

—John Quincy Adams, former U.S. president

I once read a story about three great NFL coaches: Tom Landry, Chuck Noll and Bill Walsh. These men shared a very interesting record on the way to their combined nine Superbowl wins from 1974 to 1989. They held the record for the worst first season as NFL coaches. Had they said after their first year, "I'm in the wrong vocation," they would never have known fame and success. Quitting is a universal problem. When we hit a roadblock, human nature tells us to try to get around it or retreat. It is occasionally a wise decision to re-evaluate one's direction at a roadblock, but most of the time, it's only one of many hurdles over which we must jump in order to reach the finish line.

Mark Twain phrased this principle memorably. He said that if a cat sits on a hot stove lid, it won't sit on a hot stove lid again, but it also won't sit on a cold one anymore. And therein lies the problem. Just when we need to get up from being knocked down, we say, "I'm not trying that again—look what happened last time!"

Success is the ability to go from one failure to another with no loss of enthusiasm.

—Winston Churchill, former British prime minister, statesman and author

The world of sports also teaches us not to treat losing lightly. Managers and coaches don't want players who shrink from a challenge. They want players with resolve, who don't lose all of their effectiveness when they mess up. If I played a hard game and then lost, I was naturally upset. The important skill I had to learn was to deal with my grief or disappointment, try to evaluate why the loss occurred and then turn around and focus on the next game. We need to critique past performance, but never let it drag us backwards emotionally.

 Forget about the consequences of failure. Failure is only a temporary change in direction to set you straight for your next success.

—Dennis Waitley, American productivity consultant

 Man is not the creature of circumstances. Circumstances are the creatures of men.

—Benjamin Disraeli, 19th-century British prime minister and novelist

During my NHL career, the teams that I played for had a number of different sports psychologists. One of these men, Wayne Halliwell, said something that has stuck in my mind. He talked about "park and ride." Park yesterday's loss, and ride toward tomorrow's opportunity. The challenge is not whether you have a tough problem to deal with, but whether it's the same problem you had last year.

Another psychologist emphasized the four most important words in the world: "if only" and "next time." Many people live in the if-only zone: "If only I had studied ... If only I had applied myself in that job interview ... If only I had said the right thing."

We've all done it. The problem with "if only" is that it keeps us focussed on the past.

The solution is to turn all of our "if onlys" into "next times." "Next time, I will pass that exam because I will study harder!" "Next time" closes out the failures of the past and keeps our focus on the success opportunity of the future.

A man does what he must—in spite of personal consequences, in spite of obstacles and dangers and pressures—and that is the basis of all human morality.

—John Fitzgerald Kennedy, former U.S. president

In my life, I have never viewed anything as failure, just temporary setbacks.

—Bill Marriott, American businessman

Albert Einstein's teachers saw him as shy and slow of speech, a student who would never give the right answers to their questions, and they felt that he was sometimes stupid. Looking over at a daydreaming Albert, his teacher told him, "Einstein, you will never amount to anything." What if Albert had responded by saying, "If only I could have pleased my teachers," and wallowed in memories of his unsuccessful experience at school? At the age of 26, while an unknown clerk in the Swiss patent office, he published his special theory of relativity. Twenty years later, it was said that his theory was so difficult that only 10 men in the whole world could understand it.

The Australian coat of arms contains two animals: the emu and the kangaroo. Australia became a forced destination for British prisoners, and these two animal species are most emblematic of the prisoners' fate. Neither can move backwards. The emu, with its three-toed feet, won't, and the kangaroo, with its big tail, can't. For these animals, moving forward is the only option. Prisoners arrived at the isolated continent of Australia (then a British colony called New South Wales) with a one-way ticket. Avoid the tendency to look back at defeat, which only saps away energy. Remember the emu and the kangaroo. These animals, capable of great speed, move only one way—the right way: forward.

Doubt sees the obstacles, Faith sees the way.
Doubt sees the darkest night, Faith sees the day.
Doubt dreads to take a step, Faith soars on high.
Doubt questions, "Who believes?" Faith answers, "I."

—Author Unknown

Keep your enthusiasm through tough times by dealing with failure, not personalizing it. A failed project is not a failed person. Keep climbing out of the emotional pit of failure. Recognize that all men and women face difficulties and fail.

Virtually nothing comes out right the first time. Repeated failures are the finger posts on the road to achievement.

—Charles F. Kettering, American inventor and social philosopher

The British ballet dancer Margot Fonteyn said, "The one important thing I have learned over the years is the difference between taking one's work seriously and taking one's self seriously. The first is imperative and the second is disastrous!"

Ann Landers reminded us that life will come at us. "Let's look trouble in the eye and say, 'You're not going to defeat me!'"

There is no doubt in my mind that there are many ways to be a winner, but there is really only one way to be a loser, and that is to fail and not look beyond the failure.

—Kyle Rote Jr., American soccer player and sports agent

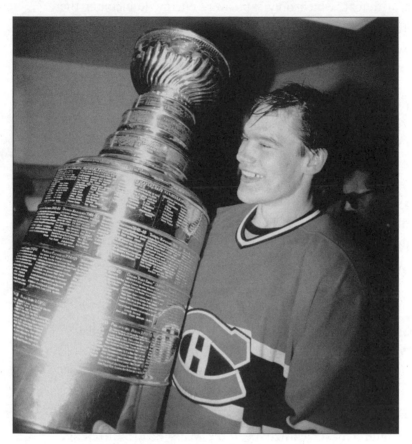

Ryan with the Stanley Cup in 1986.

Chapter 8 **Be a Hero:**
Change Today to Impact Tomorrow

One of the illusions of life is that the present hour is not the critical, decisive hour. Write it on your heart that everyday is the best day of the year.

—Ralph Waldo Emerson, American philosopher and poet

IN HIS BOOK *The Hero with a Thousand Faces*, Joseph Campbell says, "The adventure of the hero normally follows the pattern: a separation from the world, a penetration to some source of power and a life-enhancing return." His definition is a good one. As we finish our time together in these pages, we need to ask ourselves, in essence, "What life-enhancing personal change will we make today to enhance tomorrow's journey?"

Pursue heroism. The story of a child named Shay demonstrates how changed actions and attitudes can help another's journey:

> At a fundraising dinner for a school that serves children with physical and mental disabilities, the father of one of the students delivered a speech unlikely to be forgotten by any who attended. After extolling the school and its dedicated staff, he offered a question: "When not interfered with by outside

influences, everything nature does is done with perfection. Yet my son, Shay, cannot learn things as other children do. He cannot understand things as other children do. Where is the natural order of things in my son?" The audience was stilled by the query. The father continued: "I believe that when a child like Shay, physically and mentally handicapped, comes into the world, an opportunity to realize true human nature presents itself, and it comes in the way other people treat that child."

Then he told the following story: Shay and his father walked past a park where some boys Shay knew were playing baseball. Shay asked, "Do you think they'll let me play?"

His father knew that most of the boys would not want someone like Shay on their team, but the father also understood that if his son were allowed to play, it would give him a much-needed sense of belonging and some confidence to be accepted by others in spite of his limitations. Shay's father approached one of the boys on the field and asked if Shay could play, not expecting much. The boy looked around for guidance and a few boys nodded approval. So the young player took matters into his own hands and said, "We're losing by six runs, and the game is in the eighth inning. I guess he can be on our team and we'll try to put him in to bat in the ninth inning." Shay struggled over to the team's bench and put on a team shirt with a broad smile; his father had a tear in his eye and warmth in his heart. The boys saw the father's joy.

In the bottom of the eighth inning, Shay's team scored a few runs but was still behind by three. At the top of the ninth inning, Shay put on a glove and played in right field. Even though no hits went his way, he was obviously ecstatic just to be in the game and on the field. He grinned from ear to ear as his father waved to him from the stands. At the bottom of the ninth inning, Shay's team scored again. Now, with two outs and the bases loaded, the potential winning run was on base and Shay was scheduled to be next at bat. At this juncture, did they let him bat and give away their chance to win the game? Surprisingly, Shay was given the bat.

Everyone knew that a hit was all but impossible, because Shay didn't even know how to hold the bat properly, much less connect with the ball. However, as Shay stepped up to the plate, the pitcher, recognizing the other team was putting winning aside for this moment in Shay's life, moved in a few steps to lob the ball in softly so Shay might at least be able to make contact. The first pitch came and Shay swung clumsily and missed. The pitcher again took a few steps forward to toss the ball softly toward Shay. As the pitch floated in, Shay swung at the ball, and he hit a slow grounder right back to the pitcher, who easily picked it up. But instead of throwing the ball to the first baseman for an easy out, the pitcher threw it right over the head of the first baseman and out of reach of all his teammates.

Everyone in the stands and from both teams benches started yelling, "Shay, run to first! Run to first!" Never in his life had Shay run that far, but he made it to first base. He scampered down the baseline, wide-eyed and startled. Everyone yelled, "Run to second, run to second!" Catching his breath, Shay awkwardly ran toward second, gleaming and struggling to make it. By then the right fielder had the ball; he was the smallest guy on his team, and now he had a chance to be a hero for the first time. He could have thrown the ball to the second baseman for the tag, but he understood the pitcher's intentions. He intentionally threw the ball high over the third baseman's head.

Shay rounded second base and started toward third deliriously as the runners ahead of him circled the bases toward home. Everyone was screaming, "Shay, Shay, Shay! All the way, Shay!" When Shay seemed unsure which way to go, the opposing shortstop ran to help him and turned him in the direction of third base, shouting, "Run to third! Shay, run to third!" As Shay rounded third, both teams and all those watching were on their feet, screaming, "Shay, run home!" Shay ran to home, stepped on the plate and was cheered as the hero who hit the "grand slam" and won the game for his team.

"That day," said the father softly, with tears now rolling down his face, "the boys from both teams helped bring a piece of true love and humanity into this world." Shay didn't make it to another summer. He died that winter, but he never forgot being the hero and making his father so happy.

—Variations of this story have been published, but the original is attributed to Rabbi Paysach Krohn, whose "Perfection at the Plate" appeared in his book *Echoes of the Maggid* [Mesorah Publications, 1999]

Life is not only about becoming heroes ourselves, it is also about developing an atmosphere where we can help others *become heroes* too. This is what I want to focus on as we draw to the close of this book. Life is not just lived to live. Life is about finding and fulfilling our unique purpose, changing mankind's landscape!

Heroes constantly look for ways to develop their skills, take in new information, develop a new perspective (as the young player did in the above story) and create personal change for one reason ... to slay the dragon, to save the damsel in distress to ... in a nutshell, serve the Shays in our lives. Heroes recognize the need to temporarily create separation and personal growth. Heroes realize that we are human *beings* first and then humans *doing*. What we accomplish always comes primarily from who we are; thus, it is critical to see ourselves through the lenses of the previous seven chapters.

Heroes make time and find ways to grow in each of the seven areas covered in chapters 1 to 7, regardless of their position in the limelight or personal gain. Heroes have a plan to grow themselves, to take action toward their desired outcomes and, at the end of the day, they ponder right and wrong and as often as possible choose what's right for only one reason—to improve the plight of others.

I believe that long-time NHL coach Pat Quinn is right when he says, "Everyone says there's no 'I' in team, but there is. It's a big 'I,' but that 'I' has to be one that now builds. You have to have self-esteem. You have to be proud of your work. You have to be able to look in the mirror and say, 'I am accountable; I am the one that can work with these guys to accomplish a common goal.'"

Throughout this book we have looked at personal success strategies to keep our "I" on track, advancing toward all that we desire to be in order to *be a hero*, to help others accomplish their dreams. Heroes realize that all of life is preparation for fulfilling their life purpose. They are open to change and changing themselves and recognize that adjustments must be made because heroes also recognize, according to Joseph Campbell, their failings and faults.

The previous seven chapters have laid out foundational principles that help us evaluate our personal progress. As we begin to pull the drawstrings together on this information, where do you, as tomorrow's *hero*, see your greatest developmental need? If your wheel is "bumping" forward, this begs the question, "Are you committed to developing certain areas to smooth out your life ride?" Use the following quick self-assessment to create a potential starting place for the personal change that you desire to go for! In each of the categories, for example, if you feel like you're a 6 out of 10 in that area, pencil in the area up to 6 to create a visual indicator that will help chart your growth.

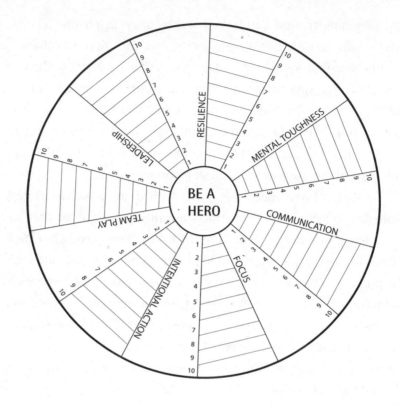

Nicely done! Potential heroes in our fast-paced world seldom take this first step of personal evaluation. The key to creating personal change is to recognize where you are and develop a "go-forward" list of how to get yourself to the next level in each of the seven categories. For example, in the area of mental toughness, if you gave yourself a 6 out of 10 on the wheel, you may choose self-talk as an area you need to improve in order to advance to the next level. Then, next to these areas of improvement, place the specific action steps that will intentionally help you accomplish this change.

Mental Toughness

_____

_____

_____

Communication

_____

_____

_____

Focus

_____

_____

_____

Intentional Action

_____

_____

_____

Team Play

_____

_____

_____

Leadership

_____

_____

_____

Resilience

_____

_____

_____

One key to making significant personal change is to make sure that we are not over-influenced by people who may slow down that change.

Processionary caterpillars travel in long, undulating lines, one creature behind the other. Jean Henri Fabre, the French entomologist, once led a group of these caterpillars onto the rim of a large flowerpot so' that the leader of the procession found himself nose to tail with the last caterpillar in the procession, forming a circle without end or beginning. Through sheer force of habit and instinct, the ring of caterpillars circled the flowerpot for seven days and seven nights, until they died from exhaustion and starvation. An ample supply of food was close at hand and plainly visible, but it was outside the range of the circle, so the caterpillars continued along the beaten path.
—Variations of this recounting have been published, but the original is attributed to broadcaster Earl Nightingale.

We often behave in a similar way. Habitual thought patterns become deeply established, and it seems easier and more comforting to follow them than to cope with change, even when that change may represent freedom, achievement and success. By focussing on our go-forward momentum in these areas, we can resist following other people's expectations for our lives. People expand possibilities and opportunities when trusted, but they contract or conserve energy when controlled.

"Tiny" Freyberg was one of the greatest fighting generals of the Second World War. He was 6 feet 2 inches tall and a big man in every way—too big to let rank come between him and his troops. Rather than saluting him, his soldiers simply called out warmly, "Hiya, Tiny!" and Freyberg always shouted back, "Hello, boys!" Tiny Freyberg never demanded his men's respect but earned it with courage and compassion. He would always be found commanding not from the rear but up near the front, usually sitting cross-legged on top of a tank. He played a major role in the battles of El Alamein, Tripoli and Trieste, among others, and once refused an order to escape with his staff to Egypt from Greece in 1941, remaining with his rear guard until all of his troops could be evacuated. He was a strict disciplinarian, putting his men through the most rigorous training to prepare them for combat, but at the same was sensitive and compassionate.

When on leave, Freyberg devoted much of his time to visiting the wounded. If a young soldier told him he'd been hit in the side, Freyberg replied, "So was I," and pulled up his shirt to display the scar. If a man had a knee wound, up went the general's trouser leg. But when he came to a man who was badly hurt, Freyberg would sit talking quietly to the soldier with genuine anguish on his face. Once, a soldier woke up on an operating table to find the general himself gripping his hand and murmuring, "You're going to be all right, lad."

A First World War Victoria Cross recipient, Freyberg emerged from the Second World War as one of Britain's most decorated heroes and the youngest brigadier in the British army. Winston Churchill nicknamed Freyberg "the Salamander" and recounted asking to see his war wounds: "He stripped and I counted 27 separate scars and gashes." In contrast, Sir James Barrie described his friend Freyberg as "Peter Pan grown up." Freyberg's modesty, generosity and general good nature combined with that fearless courage explains why the 30,000 men in his command worshipped him.

No detail affecting his troops was too minor for his attention. He often said, "Morale is a lot of little things," and he made sure that rations, mail deliveries, sports and even concerts were provided for those under his command. It was his idea to equip his division with a mobile bakery, the only one in the Eighth Army. Tiny Freyberg had a purpose, was passionate, deeply cared about others and left his hero's mark on mankind.

You may be thinking, as you read this chapter, "I never get the opportunity to be a hero!" Let's be realistic. Most of us in this world might think this hero stuff is for generals or for the rich and famous. But every one of us has the opportunity to make a difference.

Here is a story of a simple opportunity that any one of us could have jumped on:

When I was quite young, my father had one of the first telephones in our neighbourhood. I remember the polished old case fastened to the wall. The shiny receiver hung on the side of the box. I was too little to reach the telephone but used to listen with fascination when my mother talked to it.

Then I discovered that somewhere inside the wonderful device lived an amazing person. Her name was "Information Please" and there was nothing she did not know. Information Please could supply anyone's number and the correct time.

My personal experience with the genie-in-a-bottle came one day while my mother was visiting a neighbour. Amusing myself at the tool bench in the basement, I whacked my finger with a hammer. The pain was terrible, but there seemed no point in crying because there was no one home to give sympathy.

I walked around the house sucking my throbbing finger, finally arriving at the stairway. The telephone! Quickly, I ran for the footstool in the parlour and dragged it to the landing. Climbing up, I unhooked the receiver and held it to my ear. "Information, please," I said into the mouthpiece just above my head. A click or two and a small, clear voice spoke into my ear: "Information."

"I hurt my finger ..." I wailed into the phone. The tears came readily enough now that I had an audience.

"Isn't your mother home?" came the question.

"Nobody's home but me," I blubbered.

"Are you bleeding?" the voice asked.

"No," I replied. "I hit my finger with the hammer and it hurts."

"Can you open the icebox?" she asked.

I said I could.

"Then chip off a little bit of ice and hold it to your finger," said the voice.

After that, I called Information Please for everything. I asked her for help with my geography, and she told me where Philadelphia was. She helped me with my math. She told me that my pet chipmunk that I had caught in the park just the day before would eat fruit and nuts.

Then there was the time Petey, our pet canary, died. I called Information Please and told her the sad story. She listened and then said things grown-ups say to soothe a child. But I was not consoled. I asked her, "Why is it that birds should sing so beautifully and bring joy to all families, only to end up as a heap of feathers on the bottom of a cage?"

She must have sensed my deep concern, for she said quietly, "Always remember that there are other worlds to sing in."

Somehow I felt better.

Another day I was again on the telephone: "Information, please."

"Information," said the now familiar voice.

"How do I spell 'fix'?" I asked.

All this took place in a small town in the Pacific Northwest. When I was nine years old, we moved across the country to Boston. I missed my friend very much. Information Please belonged in that old wooden box back home, and I somehow never thought of trying the shiny new phone that sat on the table in the hall. As I grew into my teens, the memories of those childhood conversations never really left me.

Often, in moments of doubt and perplexity, I would recall the serene sense of security I had then. I appreciated now how patient, understanding and kind she was to have spent her time on a little boy.

A few years later, on my way west to college, my plane put down in Seattle. I had about a half hour between planes. I spent 15 minutes or so on the phone with my sister, who lives there now. Then, without thinking what I was doing, I dialled my hometown operator and said, "Information, please."

Miraculously, I heard the small, clear voice I knew so well: "Information."

I hadn't planned this, but I heard myself saying, "Could you please tell me how to spell 'fix'?"

There was a long pause. Then came the soft-spoken answer, "I guess your finger must have healed by now."

I laughed. "So it's really you," I said. "I wonder if you have any idea how much you meant to me during that time?"

"I wonder," she said, "if you know how much your calls meant to me. I never had any children, and I used to look forward to your calls."

I told her how often I had thought of her over the years, and I asked if I could call her again when I came back to visit my sister.

"Please do," she said. "Just ask for Sally."

Three months later I was back in Seattle. A different voice answered: "Information."

I asked for Sally.

"Are you a friend?" she said.

"Yes, a very old friend," I answered.

"I'm sorry to have to tell you this," she said. "Sally had been working part-time the last few years because she was sick. She died five weeks ago."

Before I could hang up she said, "Wait a minute, what did you say your name was?"

I told her.

"Well, Sally left a message for you. She wrote it down in case you called. Let me read it to you."

The note said, "Tell him there are other worlds to sing in. He'll know what I mean. Growth is the only evidence of life."

I thanked her and hung up. I knew what Sally meant.

— Variations of this story have been published, but the original is attributed to *Reader's Digest*, June 1966

Many of the world's great heroes have weighed in with sage advice about opportunity.

Thomas Edison: Opportunity is missed by most because it is dressed in overalls and looks like work.

Steven Covey: Effective people are not problem-minded; they're opportunity-minded. They feed opportunities and starve problems.

Helen Keller: When one door of happiness closes, another opens; but often we look so long at the closed door that we do not see the one which has been opened for us.

Albert Einstein: In the middle of every difficulty lies opportunity.

John F. Kennedy: The Chinese use two brush strokes to write the word 'crisis.' One brush stroke stands for danger, the other for opportunity.

Opportunities to be tomorrow's hero may be waiting for us right around today's corner. A hero's work is always internal first. As we grow ourselves and better understand our purpose and passion, our peripheral vision picks up on opportunities to serve mankind and make a difference. Recognizing opportunities is a developed skill. In the words of Tom Brokaw, "It's easy to make a buck. It's a lot tougher to make a difference."

Sometimes the toughest times bring the most opportunity. Heroes are not just soldiers or fictional characters or professional athletes. Tomorrow's heroes are people like you and me who have difficulties in life but choose to muster the courage to learn life lessons, make small adjustments and take some forward-moving action steps toward making life better for other people. Courage is not the absence of fear but working through issues and taking action despite the fear that we feel. These are the steps of heroes.

Heroes are moms and dads and janitors and police officers and firefighters and fishermen and minor sports coaches and pickup baseball players and your friends and my children and in the end ... people like you. You are a hero! Continue developing the hero in you today to have a significant impact on the world that desperately needs you tomorrow.

Ryan returns home to be assistant captain of the Vancouver Canucks, 1991–93.

Overtime **Inside an NHL Dressing Room**

I want to end our time together by asking you to follow me into our NHL dressing room during the Stanley Cup playoffs. Inside, we are readying for tonight's game. Some of us are curving and taping our sticks; some are finishing up medical treatments prior to getting dressed, and others are well into their pre-game routine.

Now the coaching staff is bringing us together for a snapshot look at the other team and an overview of the adjustments that we must make for tonight's game.

Finally, we have most of our equipment on and are on our own as a group of professional athletes, helping each other create an atmosphere that will focus us toward success. It is now the last few minutes before the game, and we are voicing our well-worn phrases that remind one another of the principles of successful competition. Words and emotion pull the team together, moving us toward a state that will give us optimum performance.

"LET'S NOT BEAT OURSELVES TONIGHT, BOYS!"

We must oversee the areas of the game that are under our control. How and when players change at the bench, how the team breaks out of its own end and forechecks the opponent are some of the hundreds of seemingly insignificant details that must be controlled to make significant impact in a game.

This phrase, "Let's not beat ourselves tonight, boys!" has real significance in professional sports and in life! Most games in life are lost, not won. But it doesn't have to be that way. Poor personal preparation and laziness account for reduced personal performance. Focussing on the areas and details of life that are in our control, and worrying less about things that are beyond our control, will enable each of us to attain a higher winning percentage.

"COME ON, BOYS! LET'S NOT JUST TALK ABOUT IT!"

Sometimes, in the game of life, we talk boldly in the dressing room among friends and colleagues but have trouble moving beyond talk to the action stage. Teams move toward their goals when individuals within the team become personally accountable for what they think, say, see and do. Successful people spend much time in preparation but never get stuck there. Massive, intelligent action is always needed to accomplish massive things. Developing a healthy capacity to find and expend energy in focussed action will bring us all closer to our Stanley Cups. Think, talk, see and then do!

"FIND A WAY TO WIN TONIGHT, BOYS, JUST FIND A WAY TO WIN!"

All of sport and life is built on our ability to choose. Much of winning is about "willing" to win. Most nights, in the National Hockey League, games come down to, "Who wants it more?" We must choose how much we are willing to sacrifice, how big a price we are willing to pay for the win. Competition is stimulating. Finding a way to win includes the technical adjustments that teams and players make to increase their opportunity for success. People finding a way to beat a debilitating disease or an onerous circumstance lead the way for the rest of us. Developing stick-to-itiveness and enthusiasm for life prepares us for both the valley and mountaintop experiences.

"GET OUR 'A-GAME' ON THE ICE TONIGHT, BOYS! LET'S GIVE OURSELVES A CHANCE TO WIN!"

If we are in the business of living (and we will be until our last breath), why not prepare to be the very best that we can be? Why wouldn't we develop a plan to increase our mental toughness, focus, communication and action? Why not build the confidence and enthusiasm that will endure and help us excel? Why not give our best effort and choose to make the best decisions for our family and our team? We all live a unique life in a unique arena, but every person is, in some way, part of a team. Why wouldn't we want to commit to being the very best teammate possible to our spouse, our co-workers and our community? Why not be a hero?

In getting our "A-game" out of the dressing room and onto our ice surface, let's commit our lives to being winners. When times are tough, our teammates can count on our never-ending enthusiasm and perseverance. We know that there will be bumps in the road and that our team will not win every time we lace up the skates. But from now on, that will not deter us. We recognize the power in our perseverance, and we know that our dogged determination is the most important ingredient in the recipe for success.

Our talk is finished. The buzzer sounds. As a team, we rise enthusiastically with one last cheer of encouragement. Adrenalin is rushing with every accelerated heartbeat. We move in a line down the tunnel toward our bench, restless now, anxious to execute on the ice what we have just heard, voiced and visualized. Prepared for the next challenge and ready to compete, we jump off the bench and into the *game!*

References

Bassham, Lanny. *With Winning in Mind*. Wilsonville, OR: Book Partners Inc., 1995.

Campbell, Joseph. *The Hero with a Thousand Faces*. Princeton, NJ: Princeton University Press, 1972.

Covey, Stephen R. *First Things First*. New York: Simon and Schuster Inc., 1994.

Cox, Valerie. "The Cookie Thief." In *A Third Serving of Chicken Soup for the Soul*, Jack Canfield and Mark Victor Hansen. Deerfield Beach, FL: Health Communications Inc., 1996.

Hayward, Steven F. *Churchill On Leadership: Executive Success in the Face of Adversity*. New York: Random House, Inc., Crown Publishing Group, 1998.

Holtz, Lou. *Winning Every Day: The Game Plan for Success*. New York HarperCollins Publishers Inc., HarperBusiness, 1998.

Jamison, Steve. *A True North. In Wooden: A Lifetime of Observations and Reflections On and Off the Court*, John Wooden and Steve Jamison. Chicago NTC Contemporary Publishing Group Inc., Contemporary Books, 1997.

Jones, Charles E. *Life Is Tremendous*. Carol Stream, IL: Tyndale House Publishers Inc., Living Books, 1968.

Kehoe, John. *Mind Power into the 21st Century: Techniques to Harness the Astounding Powers of Thought*. Montreal: Zoetic Inc., 1997.

Maxwell, John C. *100 Lessons on Leadership*. Nashville: Thomas Nelson, Inc., 1998.

——. *The Winning Attitude: Your Key to Personal Success*. Nashville Thomas Nelson, Inc., 1993.

——. *The Success Journey*. Nashville: Thomas Nelson, Inc., 1997.

——. *The 21 Irrefutable Laws of Leadership*. Nashville: Thomas Nelson, Inc., 1998.

Miller, Saul. *Performing Under Pressure*. Toronto: McGraw-Hill Ryerson, 1992.

Morris, Tom. *True Success: A New Philosophy of Excellence*. New York: Penguin Group (USA), Berkley Books, 1995.

Phillips, Donald T. *Lincoln on Leadership: Executive Strategies for Tough Times.* New York: Warner Books Inc., 1992.

Riley, Pat. *The Winner Within.* New York: Penguin Group (USA), Berkley Books, 1993.

Seligman, Martin. *Learned Optimism: How to Change Your Mind and Your Life.* New York: Knopf, 1990.

Short, Bo. *The Foundation of Leadership: Enduring Principles to Govern Our Lives.* London: Excalibur Press, 1997.

Sweeting, George. *Great Quotes and Illustrations.* Waco, TX: Word Books, 1985.

Waitley, Denis. *Seeds of Greatness: The Ten Best-Kept Secrets of Total Success.* Old Tappan, NJ: Revell, 1983.

Wooden, John, and Steve Jamison. *Wooden: A Lifetime of Observations and Reflections On and Off the Court.* Chicago: NTC/Contemporary Publishing Group Inc., Contemporary Books, 1997.

Ziglar, Zig. *How to Be A Winner.* Niles, IL: Nightingale-Conant Corp, 1990.

——. *How to Be A Winner.* New York: Simon & Schuster Audio; Nightingale Conant Corp, 1995.

Thanks ...

This book is all about coaching people to reach their highest potential. I want to take this opportunity to thank my on-ice coaches who have, for many years, inspired and nurtured me along my journey.

It is significant that my father is at the top of the minor-hockey list below. My earliest hockey memories include involvement from Mom and Dad.

MINOR HOCKEY Bill Walter, John Magill, Cliff Betts, George Wong, Red Gladson, Gus Kearns, Bob Okranitz

JUNIOR HOCKEY Gill Lundin, Ron Livingston, Harvey Roy, Ivan Prediger, Les Calder

NHL Tom McVie, Dan Belisle, Gary Green, Brian Murray, Bob Berry, Jacques Lemaire, Jacques Laperrière, Jean Perron, Pat Burns, Pat Quinn, Ron Wilson, Rick Lee, Stan Smyl, Glen Hanlon, Yvon Labre, Charles Thiffault

The glory of sport comes from dedication, determination and desire. Achieving success and personal glory in athletics has less to do with wins and losses than it does with learning how to prepare yourself so that at the end of the day, whether on the track or in the office, you know that there was nothing more you could have done to reach your ultimate goal.

—Jackie Joyner-Kersee, American heptathlete

www.ryanwalter.com

Check out the website as an online extension to this book.

- Ryan's expanded life story
- Off the Bench study connected to the Scriptures
- Ryan's free weekly e-newsletter, "Staying and Playing HUNGRY"
  ... and much much more!

Interested in having Ryan speak to your team, company or organization?

Visit **www.ryanwalter.com** for more information and to connect directly with Ryan.

About the Author

Ryan Walter grew up playing hockey in Burnaby, British Columbia, and like many Canadian boys had dreams of one day playing in the National Hockey League. He scored 30 goals in his first year of junior hockey, playing for the Langley Lords at age 15. In his final year with Seattle, while attending college part-time and learning to tie flies and fish steelhead, he scored 54 goals and 71 assists, became the Western Hockey League's most valuable player and representative at the Memorial Cup championship, was named captain of Canada's World Junior Team and was selected second overall in the 1978 entry draft by the Washington Capitals. During his four seasons in Washington, while still attending college part-time, he was named the youngest captain in NHL history, scored 38 goals in his fourth and final season with the Caps and played for Team Canada at four straight World Championships.

The Montreal *Gazette's* "Worst trade in NHL History" headline heralded a great move to the Montreal Canadiens for Ryan and his wife, Jennifer. In 1983 Ryan was selected to play in the All-Star game, and in 1986 he helped the legendary Canadiens win hockey's greatest trophy, the Stanley Cup. After nine great seasons playing for the Habs, having four children, learning French and being elected vice-president of the NHL Players' Association, he returned to B.C. to play his last two seasons for the Vancouver Canucks. His parents, who had been so supportive throughout his career, were able to go to all his home games for the first time since he played junior hockey in Langley. In his final season with the Canucks, he played in his 1,000th game and was named NHL Man of the Year.

Today, Ryan has a master's degree in leadership/business, has been the founding partner in two start-up companies, is the author of three books and creator of the board game Trade Deadline™. He can be seen on television as a hockey analyst for Rogers Sportsnet and Canucks pay-per-view games, as an expert on the television series *Making the Cut* and on the big screen as a referee in the movie *Miracle*.

Ryan's adrenalin rush now comes from motivating others with speeches, interactive leadership sessions and corporate coaching as he pursues his mission of inspiring the hungry spirit. But his greatest satisfaction of all is simply being husband to Jennifer and father to Ben, Christy, Ryan, Joe and Emma.

Praise for *Off the Bench and Into the Game*

"The principles for success that Ryan outlines within this book are timeless and know no boundaries. Whether your team be your family, the Montreal Canadiens, or a high tech engineering and sales team, I believe these principles are the foundations required for high performance and extraordinary achievement."
—Joe Pajer, executive vice-president and general manager, Marconi Communications

"Ryan's ability to separate the important from the trivial, and support it with clear, easy to understand life experiences is just marvelous. He shines light on many murky areas, showing us how to reach our goals and succeed."
— Bob Gainey, executive vice-president and general manager, Montreal Canadiens

"Ryan Walter's book is a must-read for any executive inside or outside of sport. This is a critically useful tool for any athlete who is trying to maximize his or her athletic ability. Finally, this is an inspirational read for any young person trying to sort things out. Ryan Walter was a great leader as a player, setting a high standard with his intelligence and work ethic. He has a lot to offer to people trying to sharpen their skills in these areas."
—Brian Burke, executive vice-president and general manager, Anaheim Ducks

"*Off the Bench and Into the Game* is the story of the author. Ryan Walter is an example of all that he writes about in this book. Authenticity is a major factor for me. When you read this book you are getting the real thing. When Ryan talks about being mentally tough and making the right choices, you are hearing from someone who lives that kind of character-driven life. You will enjoy the great stories and illustrations that make this book an exciting, inspirational and informative read."
—James E. Janz, president, Janz and Associates

"Ryan Walter, the NHL hockey player, analyst, coach, entrepreneur, husband and father, has captured key principles for life and leadership. These principles are well illustrated with anecdotes and experiences from his life and career. *Off the Bench and Into the Game* is a tremendous resource for anyone who wants to stand in the winner's circle in the game of life."
—Don Liesemer, president, Hockey Ministries International